THE CIVIL WAR
IN
WEST VIRGINIA
A PICTORIAL HISTORY
BY
STAN COHEN

Gateway Printing & Litho.
Missoula, Montana
1976

i

Library of Congress Number 76-2880
Printed in the U.S.A.
Copyright © by Stan Cohen, Pictorial Histories
4103 Virginia Ave. S.E.
Charleston, West Virginia 25304

*DEDICATED TO ALL
WEST VIRGINIANS
AND ESPECIALLY TO MY MOTHER*

TABLE OF CONTENTS

MAP INDEX

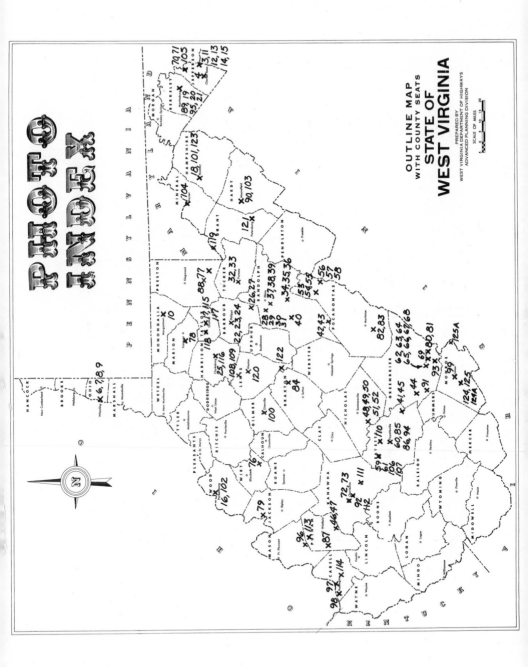

PHOTO INDEX

OUTLINE MAP
WITH COUNTY SEATS
STATE OF
WEST VIRGINIA

PREPARED BY
WEST VIRGINIA DEPARTMENT OF HIGHWAYS
ADVANCED PLANNING DIVISION

SCALE OF MILES
5 0 5 10 15 20

Union soldiers from Ritchie County. Courtesy of WVU Library Archives.

FOREWARD

One has only to travel through the West Virginia countryside to appreciate the difficulties the Civil War soldier had in waging war there. Although the state was not the scene of major battles that shaped the outcome of the war (except perhaps for Harpers Ferry in 1862), the occurrence of more than 600 minor battles, skirmishes and raids between 1861 and 1865 showed that both North and South considered West Virginia a vital piece of real estate.

It was brother against brother, neighbor against neighbor in this theater of war. The state furnished some 30,000 troops to the Union and from 7,000 to 9,000 to the Confederacy. The state was one of the highest in percentage of total population enlisting as Federal troops. These soldiers fought near their homes and in every distant zone of the war.

Many more men and a few women were in the home guards and local partisan units and some fought on neither side but used the war as an excuse for killing and stealing for their own pleasure and gain.

Maps of the period show that the state was a gateway to the Ohio River and the Midwestern states if the South had control, and to the Virginia Valley if the North held sway. The mountainous terrain precluded the mass troop movements characteristic of the other theaters.

The deciding factor for both sides to consider, and it had a lot to do with the formation of West Virginia as a political entity, was the existence of two railroads: the Baltimore and Ohio in the northern part of the state, and the Virginia and Tennessee just over the border in Virginia in the south. These railroads were the lifeblood of both sides.

Since the state was a buffer between north and south, the first military actions of the war occurred here. And there were other firsts of the Civil War (and in some instances of modern warfare) such as: the military use of telegraph, indirect artillery fire, first Union and Confederate soldiers killed, first General killed and an oil field destroyed.

I have tried in this book to trace the highlights of the war through pictures of sites as they look now and as they looked then. Time and people have not been kind to many sites. Nevertheless, much of the past remains. I hope this book will give the West Virginian and the Civil War buff from outside the state a closer picture of events that shaped the state's history. There are many good books available to the reader who wants to explore events in more detail.

I wish to thank the following for making this book possible: Bill McNeel of the Pocahontas Times in Marlinton; Walter Leach, superintendent of Carnifex Ferry Battlefield State Park; Miss Genevieve Smith of Beverly; Miss Mary Jenkins, librarian at the State Archives in Charleston; Bruce Graham of S. Spencer Moore Company in Charleston; Bob Hart of Belington; Tom Ryan of Fayetteville; R.H. Bowman of Rainelle; Rodney Pyles and Golda Riggs of the West Virginia University Library Archives; Mrs. G. Roderick Cheeseman of Boydville in Martinsburg; Jack Zinn of Nutter Fork; Mrs. Beverly Fluty of Wheeling; and Barbara McCallum and Bob McGiffert who edited my manuscript.

CHAPTER ONE

Prelude to Civil War

Although it preceded the Civil War by a year and a half, John Brown's raid on the U.S. arsenal at Harpers Ferry, Jefferson County on October 16, 1859, helped shape the war's events in the following years. Brown, a long-time advocate of abolition, wanted to arm the slaves and promote a general uprising in the South. On the night of Oct. 16 with 21 supporters, he left his Maryland hideout and attacked the arsenal in an attempt to capture weapons for the slaves. He seized a number of civilian hostages and was finally forced to seek refuge in the arsenal's firehouse. The Federal Government sent Lt. Col. Robert E. Lee with a force of Marines to crush the rebellion. Lee had as his lieutenant Jeb Stuart, who was later to become Lee's cavalry commander. Brown was captured after a brief fight on the 18th and taken to Charles Town, Jefferson County, to be tried for treason, and was hanged there on Dec. 2, 1859. He became a martyr for the abolition cause in the North. T.J. Jackson (later to be known as "Stonewall" Jackson) was in attendance at the hanging with a troop from the Virginia Military Institute. A trooper named John Wilkes Booth was another witness, as was Edmund Ruffin, an arch-secessionest from Virginia who supposedly fired the first shot of the Civil War at Fort Sumter.

It was not until Jan. 1, 1863 that the slaves were set free by President Lincoln.

Portrait of John Brown in 1859. Courtesy of the Harpers Ferry National Historical Park.

The Harpers Ferry armory firehouse where John Brown was captured on October 17, 1859. Harpers Ferry National Historical Park.

3

Jefferson County Courthouse, Charles Town where John Brown was tried and convicted of treason in 1859. Courtesy W. Va. Dept. of Commerce.

A Call to Arms, Secession, Restoration and Statehood

The firing on Fort Sumter and President Lincoln's call to arms in April 1861 set Virginia on the road to secession from the Union and membership in the Confederacy. A convention in Richmond passed a secession ordinance on April 17, 1861, and ordered it put to a vote of the people. The delegates and people of the western counties overwhelmingly voted against the ordinance and talked of leaving the mother state.

For the most part the people of the western 34 counties of Virginia had always felt apart from their eastern brothers because of the lack of money and support from the Richmond government, the differences in terrain between the two sections and the absence of slave labor in the west.

The *Wheeling Intelligencer,* which was started in 1852 and was edited by the brilliant statesman A.W. Campbell, was an early advocate of statehood and the only newspaper in Virginia to support Lincoln for President in 1860. It asked in one of its issues, "If Virginia can secede from the United States, why cannot West Virginia secede from Virginia?"

After the secession ordinance was passed, the western delegates came home and mass meetings were held throughout the region to denounce the action taken at Richmond. At the First Wheeling Convention on May 13 the foundation for statehood was laid. The Second Wheeling Convention convened on June 11 with 57 delegates in attendance. A "Restored Government of Virginia" was established with Francis H. Pierpont as the first governor. The congressmen from the "restored state" were seated in Congress, and President Lincoln recognized them. This secession from another state without that state's permission is unparalled in American history and has been questioned for constitutional legality.

The Second Wheeling Convention adopted on June 17, 1861, the following "Declaration of the People of Virginia" which is one of the most important state papers in West Virginia history:

THE TRUE PURPOSE OF ALL GOVERNMENT is to promote the welfare and provide for the protection and security of the governed, and when any form or organization of government proves inadequate for, or subversive of this purpose, it is the right, it is the duty of the latter to abolish it. The Bill of Rights of Virginia, framed in 1776, re-affirmed in 1830, and again in 1851, expressly reserves this right to a majority of her people. The act of the General Assembly, calling the Convention which assembled in Richmond in February last, without the previously expressed consent of such majority, was therefore a usurpation; and the Convention thus called has not only abused the powers nominally entrusted to it, but, with the connivance and active aid of the executive, has usurped and exercised other powers, to the manifest injury of the people, which, if permitted, will inevitably subject them to a military despotism.

The Convention, by its pretended ordinances, has required the people of Virginia to separate from and wage war against the government of the United States, and against citizens of neighboring States, with whom they have heretofore maintained friendly, social and business relations:

It has attempted to subvert the Union founded by Washington and his co-patriots, in the purer days of the republic, which has conferred unexampled prosperity upon every class of citizens, and upon every section of the country:

It has been attempted to transfer the allegiance of the people to an illegal confederacy of rebellious States, and required their submission to its pretended edicts and decrees:

It has attempted to place the whole military force and military operations of the Commonwealth under the control and direction of such confederacy, for offensive as well as defensive purposes:

It has, in conjunction with the State executive, instituted wherever their usurped power extends, a reign of terror intended to suppress the free expression of the will of the people, making elections a mockery and a fraud.

6

The same combination, even before the passage of the pretended ordinance of secession, instituted war by the seizure and appropriation of the property of the Federal Government, and by organizing and mobilizing armies, with the avowed purpose of capturing or destroying the Capital of the Union:

They have attempted to bring the allegiance of the people of the United States into direct conflict with their subordinate allegiance to the State, thereby making obedience to their pretended Ordinances, treason against the former.

We, therefore, the delegates here assembled in Convention to devise such measures and take such action as the safety and welfare of the loyal citizens of Virginia may demand, having maturely considered the premises, and viewing with great concern the deplorable condition to which this once happy Commonwealth must be reduced unless some regular adequate remedy is speedily adopted, and appealing to the Supreme Ruler of the Universe for the rectitude of our intentions, do hereby, in the name and on the behalf of the good people of Virginia, solemnly declare, that the preservation of their dearest rights and liberties and their security in person and property, imperatively demand the reorganization of the government of the Commonwealth, and that all acts of said Convention and Executive, tending to separate this Commonwealth from the United States, or to levy and carry on war against them, are without authority and void; and that the offices of all who adhere to the said Convention and Executive, whether legislative, executive or judicial, are vacated.

The "Restored Government of Virginia" gave its blessing to the formation of a new state and the first constitution was completed on Feb. 18, 1862. On April 3, 1862, the Constitution was ratified by a vote of 18,862 to 514 after some changes had been made in the provisions on slavery. On Dec. 31, 1862, President Lincoln signed a bill authorizing the admission of the new state of West Virginia, which at first was to be called Kanawha. On April 20, 1863, Lincoln issued a proclamation granting statehood effective June 20, 1863. The capital was established at Wheeling and Arthur I. Boreman was elected the first governor.

Thirty nine counties were included in the proposed state after Pocahontas, Greenbrier, Monroe, Mercer and McDowell were added to get more counties with Democratic party majorities. The Republicans did not want any former Virginia slave counties in the state, but accepted these five because the mountains in the counties gave the new state a natural barrier. The eastern panhandle counties of Pendleton, Hardy, Hampshire, Berkeley, Jefferson and Morgan, were included for protection and because of the fact that the Baltimore and Ohio Railroad wanted all of its track included in the new state's boundaries.

The last had not been heard, however, from the mother state of Virginia. She sued West Virginia in 1906 for debts unpaid after the new state took over property (the State Hospital at Weston and a few roads) on June 20, 1863. The compensation amounted to more than four million dollars in principal and more than eight million in interest. West Virginia acknowledged the debt, but final payment was not made until July 1, 1939.

1,010
BRAVE MEN
WANTED!

I am authorized by Governor Pierpoint to raise a Regiment of men to consist of

TEN COMPANIES

of 101 men each, including officers. When two companies are formed they will be mustered into service and a camp will be established at or near Morgantown, where they will be armed, equipped and drilled until the Regiment is full and ordered into service.

July 29, 1861.   JAMES EVANS.

Courtesy WVU Library Archives.

Independence Hall, Wheeling, Ohio County, site of the birth of West Virginia. It was here in 1861, the "Declaration of Rights" was adopted and the Restored Government of Virginia was established. Erected in 1859 and now being restored by the W. Va. Independence Hall Foundation. Courtesy W. Va. Dept. of Commerce.

The Custom House (Independence Hall) in 1861. Courtesy the W. Va. Independence Hall Foundation.

HARPER'S WEEKLY.

JOURNAL OF CIVILIZATION

VOL. V.—No. 236.]   NEW YORK, SATURDAY, JULY 6, 1861.   [SINGLE COPIES SIX CENTS.
[$2 50 PER YEAR IN ADVANCE.

Entered according to Act of Congress, in the Year 1861, by Harper & Brothers, in the Clerk's Office of the District Court for the Southern District of New York.

THE UNION MUST, AND SHALL BE PRESERVED

CONSTITUENT CONVENTION OF VIRGINIA, ASSEMBLED IN THE CUSTOM-HOUSE AT WHEELING, OHIO CO., JUNE, 1861.—SKETCHED BY JASPER GREEN, ESQ.—[SEE NEXT PAGE.]

Convention of Virginia, Custom House, Wheeling June 1861.
Courtesy the W. Va. Independence Hall Foundation

Store front at 1406 Main Street, Wheeling. Before and after June 20, 1863.

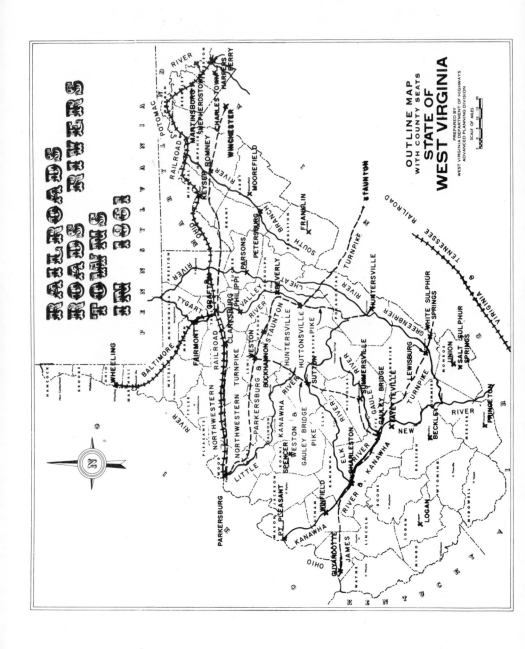

Map 1

14

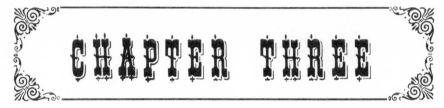

CHAPTER THREE

1861
A Year
of Strategies
and Blunders

A map of western Virginia in 1861 would show four transportation routes through the region to the northern states: the James River and Kanawha Turnpike through the Great Kanawha Valley, the Parkersburg and Staunton Turnpike through the center of the state, the Northwestern Pike following the line of present-day Route 50 and the Baltimore and Ohio Railroad in the north. These areas were fought over in 1861, and almost every action throughout the war was directly connected to one of these routes.

The governor of Virginia, John Letcher, issued two proclamations to the people of northwestern Virginia on June 14, 1861. In the first he announced adoption of the Ordinance of Secession by the Virginia voters at the election on May 23 and also proclaimed the constitution of the Provisional Government of the Confederate States of America in force throughout Virginia.

His second proclamation, which follows, appealed directly to the people of the northwest where the restoration of the Virginia government was under way at Wheeling. It was published at Huttonsville, Randolph County, and circulated in counties occupied by Southern forces:

THE SOVEREIGN PEOPLE OF VIRGINIA unbiased and by their own free choice have by a majority of nearly one hundred thousand qualified voters, severed the ties that heretofore bound them to the government of the United States, and united this Commonwealth with the Confederate States. . . . .

15

The State of Virginia has now the second time in her history asserted this right, and it is the duty of every Virginian to acknowledge her act when ratified by such majority, and to his willing co-operation to make good the declaration. All her people have voted, each has taken his chance to have his personal views represented.

You as well as the rest of the State have cast your vote fairly and the majority is against you. It is the duty of good citizens to yield to the will of the State. The bill of rights has proclaimed "that the people have a right to uniform government, and that, therefore, no government separate from or independent of the government of Virginia ought to be erected or established within the limits thereof." The majority thus declared therefore have a right to govern.

But notwithstanding this right that exercise has been regarded by the people of all sections of the United States, as undoubted, and sacred, yet the government at Washington now utterly denies it, and by the exercise of despotic power is endeavoring to coerce our people to adject submission to their authority. Virginia has asserted her independence. She will maintain it at every hazard. She is sustained by the power of her sister Southern States, ready and willing to uphold her cause. Can any true Virginian refuse to render assistance?

BALTIMORE AND OHIO RAILROAD

Perhaps the most important route through the state was the Baltimore and Ohio Railroad, which ran from Baltimore through Maryland and West Virginia to Parkersburg and Wheeling. The railroad had been built to Harpers Ferry in 1834, to Piedmont in 1851, to Fairmont in 1852, and to Wheeling in 1853. A branch line, the Northwestern Railroad from Grafton to Parkersburg, had been finished in 1857. Its tracks carried the troops and supplies for the eastern and western theaters of war. The railroad was the cause of frequent battles, raids and skirmishes, and its protection tied up thousands of Union troops. In 1864, the first mass movement of troops by railroad was achieved when 20,000 Union soldiers were detached from the eastern armies and sent to Chattanooga, Tennessee. The maneuver took several days and 400 trains.

After the Virginia Ordinance of Secession was passed, Southern Col. T.J. Jackson captured Harpers Ferry and sought to control the railroad. At the time the railroad had decided to remain neutral, but after Jackson, by a ruse, captured 56 engines and more than 300 cars, and burned most of them at Martinsburg, Berkeley County, the railroad cast its lot with the Union.

McCLELLAN TAKES COMMAND

Union men, alarmed at the southern occupation of the Kanawha Valley and the railroad junction at Grafton, Taylor County, sent an appeal to Gen. George McClellan, commander of the Department of Ohio, for assistance in protecting the railroad and the Union people in the area, McClellan hesitated to send troops, thinking the people would consider them invaders, but on May 1, 1861, he sent soldiers to Parkersburg, Benwood and Wheeling. He issued a proclamation on May 26:

"To the Union Men of Western Virginia.
    Virginians:

The general government has long enough endured the machinations of a few factious rebels in your midst. Armed traitors have in vain endeavored to deter you from expressing your loyalty at the polls. Having failed in their infamous attempts to deprive you of the exercise of your dearest rights, they now seek to inaugurate a reign of terror and thus force you to yield to their schemes and submit to the yoke of the Southern Confederacy. They are destroying the property of Citizens, and ruining your magnificent railroads. The general Government has hithertofore carefully abstained from sending troops across the Ohio, or even posting them along the banks, although frequently urged to do so by many of your prominent citizens. I determined to wait the result of the late election, desirous that no one might be able to say that the slightest effort had been made from this side to influence you in the free expression of your opinion, although many agencies were brought to bear upon you by the rebels were well known.
    "You have shown under adverse circumstances, that the great mass of the people of Western Virginia are true and loyal to the beneficent government under which we and our fathers have lived so long. As soon as the result of the election was known the traitors commenced their works of destruction. The general Government

17

cannot close its ears or eyes to the demand you have made for assistance. I have ordered troops to cross the river. They come to you as friends and brothers, as enemies to the armed rebels who are preying on you. Your homes, your families and your property are safe under their protection. All your rights shall be religiously respected.

"Notwithstanding all that has been said by the traitors to induce you to believe that our advent among you will be signalized by interference with your slaves, understand one thing clearly, not only will we abstain from such interference but we will crush any attempt at insurrection with an iron hand.

"Now that we are in your midst, I call upon you to fly to arms and support the general government, sever the connection that bind you to traitors. Proclaim to the world that faith and loyalty so long boasted by the Old Dominion is still preserved in Western Virginia and that you remain true to the stars and stripes."

On the same day McClellan addressed the soldiers who were to comprise the expedition into western Virginia:

"SOLDIERS:" You are ordered to cross the frontier and enter upon the soil of Virginia. Your mission is to restore peace and confidence, to protect the majesty of the law and to rescue our brethern from the grasp of armed traitors. You are to act in concert with the Virginia troops and support their advance. I place under the protection of your honor, the persons and property of the Virginians. I know that you will respect their feelings and their rights. Preserve the strictest discipline, remember that each one of you holds the honor of Ohio and the Union in your keeping.

"If you are called upon to overcome armed opposition I know that your courage is equal to the task, but remember that your only foes are the armed traitors, and show mercy to them when they are in your power, for many are misled. When under your protection the loyal men of Western Virginia have been enabled to organize and they can protect themselves, and then you can return to your homes with the proud satisfaction of having preserved a gallant people from destruction."

BATTLE OF PHILIPPI

Col. George Porterfield, the Confederate commander, was sent to Grafton by Gen. Lee to recruit for the Confederate Army and to take over control of the B and O Railroad, but he had little success. He retreated to Philippi, Barbour County, upon the arrival of Union troops at Grafton. The first land battle of the war was fought at Philippi on June 3 when the Federals, under Col. Benjamin F. Kelley, surprised the Confederates and caused them to retreat in disorder to Beverly, Randolph County. No one was killed in the encounter but a Union cavalryman, J.E. Hanger, had his leg shot off by a cannon ball. He later formed a company that became the world's largest makers of artificial limbs. It is still in business.

The first Union soldier killed in the war was Pvt. Thornsberry Bailey Brown, killed by a Confederate sentry at Fetterman(Grafton) on May 22, 1861.

BATTLES OF RICH MOUNTAIN AND CORRICKS FORD

After the Philippi affair, Gen. McClellan took direct command at Clarksburg, Harrison County, while Gen. Lee appointed Gen. Robert S. Garnett to take over Southern forces. Garnett fortified positions at Laurel Hill near Belington, Barbour County, and Rich Mountain near Beverly. Both positions commanded the Parkersburg and Staunton Turnpike. After some characteristic long delays McClellan moved on the positions on July 10, 1861. He sent a force to Laurel Hill to make the Confederates think the main attack was to be there, and sent Gen. William S. Rosecrans on a long flanking movement to Rich Mountain, guided by David Hart, who lived on the mountaintop. The Confederates at Rich Mountain, under Lt. Col. John Pegram, were routed and retreated toward Beverly.

Gen. Garnett, stationed at Laurel Hill with 4,000 to 6,000 men, heard of the Rich Mountain disaster and decided to retreat toward Beverly. He saw troops at Beverly, and thinking they were Federals, backtracked to the north toward Parsons, Tucker County. The troops he saw were actually his own men retreating from Rich Mountain. The Rich Mountain defenders fell back to Laurel Hill but found it abandoned and 555 men surrendered to the Federals.

At Corricks Ford in Parsons, the Confederates fought a rear-guard action, and were again defeated, losing most of their wagon train. Gen. Garnett became the first general killed in the war. The Federals abandoned the pursuit, and the Southerners continued through Maryland to Hardy and Pendleton Counties and then to Monterey, Virginia.

The engagement at Rich Mountain was of great significance to the movement to form the new state. It influenced public opinion in the Trans-Allegheny section and helped establish the authority of the Restored Government, which made the formation of the state possible.

Gen. McClellan was called to Washington to take over a larger command on July 22, 1861.

KANAWHA VALLEY CAMPAIGN

Meanwhile in the Kanawha Valley, Gen. Henry Wise, a former governor of Virginia, had occupied the valley west of Charleston, Kanawha County. The southern counties of western Virginia were more sympathetic to the southern cause than the northern counties. An advertisement in the *Kanawha Valley Star* of May 28, 1861, printed in Charleston, read:

WANTED
12,000 MEN

The convention of Virginia having passed an ordinance for the organization of a Provisional Army of able-bodied men, capable and willing to defend their homes and rights are called upon to fill its ranks. It is provided that the same pay and allowances received by the army of the North shall be given to soldiers of the Provisional army. Monthly pay: Sergeants $17; Corporals $13; Privates $11; with liberal allowances of clothing and subsistence and medical attendence free of expense.

1st Lt. L.W. Reid, Va. Forces
Recruiting Officer
Headquarters, Charleston, Kanawha County, Virginia

An advertisement appeared in the *Richmond Enquirer* for recruits for the great adventure to come:

WISE'S LEGION

We have been reliably informed that President Davis has authorized Gov. Wise to enlist a Brigade to act as a Partisan Legion, to be composed of cavalry and infantry. We predict for Wise's Legion a reputation equal to that of Lee's famous Legion of the Revolutionary War. Volunteers who wish early and active duty will do well to make prompt application to Gov. Wise at Richmond.

Arms of all kinds; rifles, doublebarrell shot-guns, sabres, and revolvers, private arms of every description, will be used by the Legion — Long range runs will not be needed, though not rejected by the Legion. Gov. Wise is not the man to stand at longrange.

All cavalry companies who desire active duty should apply immediately. This must be the great arm of the Partisan Legion.

Recruiting stations will be announced as soon as the primary organization has been completed.

RICHMOND ENQUIRER

Scary Creek on the west side of the Kanawha River near present St. Albans was occupied by a force of Confederates under the command of Col. George S. Patton, the grandfather of General George S. Patton of World War II fame. Gen. Jacob Cox of Ohio was ordered to proceed down the Kanawha Valley and dislodge the enemy from the Valley. He moved on the area from three directions and on July 17 his forces met the Confederates at the junction of Scary Creek and the Kanawha River in Putnam County. After many hours of battle, both sides retreated, but the Confederates rallied and came back to claim victory. Col. Patton was wounded in the battle. Because this was the first large-scale battle for many of the participants, both sides committed many blunders.

The Southern victory was short-lived. Upon learning of Gen. Garnett's defeat in the northwest, Wise decided his position was in danger from the east and he departed the Valley and reestablished his army in Greenbrier County. Thus the Union forces by July had control of the vital Kanawha Valley to Gauley Bridge, Fayette County.

A first sergeant in the 8th Virginia Volunteer Infantry sent to Miss Sallie Young at Teays Valley in Putnam County the following poem he had written about Wise's retreat from the Hawks Nest area. (From the Roy Bird Cook collection WVU Library Archives.)

WISE'S RETREAT FROM HAWKS NEST

Should old acquaintence be forgot
    And never brought to mind
To think old Wise had run away
    And left one hog behind

He stole away the last old goose
   He eat the - - - - - -* cow
He did not spare the - - - - - -* horse
   But left one poor old sow.

He used up all the oats and corn
   He fed up all the hay
And when the eleventh came in sight
   Old Wise he ran away

He ran so fast he could not stop
   For valley or for hill
He had no time to call around
   To pay his washing bill

And when old Gabriel blow his horn
   And the devil claim his own
May he throw wide his arms
   To welcome old Wise home

And when he takes old Wise below
   With Jenkins and his host
May he, with fear and trembling
   No longer swear and boast

When Floyd comes home to meet him
   Which he is sure to do
May the devil and his angels
   Put both the traitors through

But, good devil, be you careful
   And give them all they need
Or, by the great old Moses
   They'll get mad and secede

Watch Floyd in every movement
   Be sure to guard him well
For if you don't be careful
   He'll steal Wise out of h - ll.

* Illegible

GENERAL LEE'S CAMPAIGN

After Garnett's death Gen. Lee came to West Virginia on August 3, 1861, on a tour of inspection and consultation on the plan of campaign. His immediate purpose was to drive the Union force, commanded by Gen. John J. Reynolds, from positions at Elkwater, Randolph County, which controlled the

Huttonsville-Huntersville Pike, and from the Cheat Mountain Summit Fort on the Parkersburg and Staunton Pike. Lee had approximately 15,000 men in the area but had great difficulty because of the almost daily rainfall in August and September. Measles also took a heavy toll. Lee's campaign in this area failed in part because of the failure of his subordinate officers to give him their wholehearted support.

Lee ordered Gen. W.W. Loring to move up the road toward Huttonsville and attack the Cheat Mountain fort, but Loring waited until he could get supplies. Lee then went to Valley Mountain near Mace, Pocahontas County, on the Huttonsville Pike, to scout the area and found that the Union troops were fortifying the road. It has rained for 20 days and the road was almost impassable. On Aug. 12 Loring moved to Valley Mountain and Lee formed his plan to attack from three directions. The plan went well for a while but did not succeed partly because of a lack of coordination. The main forces that were to attack the Cheat Mountain fort thought there were 4,000 troops at the fort, when actually there were only 300, so they did not attack.

On Sept. 13, while on scouting duty at Elkwater, Col. James Washington, the last owner of Mount Vernon and an aide-de-camp to Gen. Lee, was killed by Union troops. This greatly disturbed Lee, who was a close friend of Col. Washington.

CROSS LANES-CARNIFEX FERRY-SEWELL MOUNTAIN

Gen. William S. Rosecrans had taken over as Union commander in West Virginia upon McClellan's recall to Washington. Gen. Jacob Cox held a fortified post at Gauley Bridge and patrolled the area. The Confederates, following Lee's plan, hoped to regain the Kanawha Valley, but the continuing quarrel between Gen. Wise and Gen. John Floyd, both ex-governors of Virginia and political antagonists, kept the army from being united. Floyd was overall commander in the area because of his earlier commission date, but Wise kept burdening Lee with criticisms of Floyd.

Gen. Floyd's troops attacked a force of Federals at Kesslers Cross Lanes, a few miles west of Carnifex Ferry, on Aug. 26 and completely surprised them. By this engagement the Confederates regained control of Nicholas County and cut communications with Gen. Rosecrans' headquarters in Clarksburg. Floyd then established his command on the bluffs overlooking Carnifex Ferry at Camp Gauley. Rosecrans, determined to save his army on the Kanawha, moved south and attacked Floyd on Sept. 10 at Camp Gauley. The battle lasted all day, and that night Floyd retreated from the camp to save his army from the larger enemy force. He marched to Meadow Bluff to the south in Greenbrier County where he met Lee. Rosecrans' troops took over the area and the Kanawha Valley remained in Union hands.

The Confederate command then marched to Big Sewell Mountain in Fayette County on the James River and Kanawha Turnpike and fortified positions there. On Sept. 22 Lee arrived at Sewell Mountain but could not get much information on the enemy because of the lack of cavalry and the constant battle between the two Confederate commanders. Wise was finally ordered back to Richmond and by Sept. 29 most of the Confederate force had been consolidated with Lee's troops at Sewell. Meanwhile, the Union forces had taken up positions facing Lee and for two weeks the forces opposed each other with no decisive results. With no results forthcoming Rosecrans withdrew from his positions on Oct. 5. A threatened attack west of Staunton and the cold weather kept Lee from taking advantage of the withdrawal. On Oct. 20 Lee gave up further offensive movements and ordered troops to withdraw toward Lewisburg, Greenbrier County. Lee was recalled to Virginia and thus the Trans-Allegheny Virginia area was not secured for the South.

Gen. Lee had purchased his horse, Traveller, which was to carry him through the war, while he was on Sewell Mountain. The horse had been raised near Blue Sulphur Springs in Greenbrier County. He cost Lee $200.

BATTLE OF GREENBRIER RIVER

After the campaign at Cheat Mountain the Confederates withdrew to the present town of Bartow, Pocahontas County, at the crossing of the Greenbrier River and the Parkersburg and

Staunton Turnpike. There was an inn there called Travelers' Repose, which still stands, and a fort called Camp Bartow was built behind it. Gen. John J. Reynolds, in command of Union forces in the Cheat Mountain area, sent his troops to dislodge the enemy and open up the turnpike. Although he had a superior force, the Confederates had a better position, and upon seeing reinforcements coming down the turnpike from the summit, Reynolds broke off the engagement and returned to Cheat Mountain. The battle took place on Oct. 3.

TOP OF ALLEGHENY BATTLE

An outstanding example of a Civil War campground and battlefield is well preserved at Top of Allegheny just off Route 250 in Pocahontas County. More than 4,200 feet of trenches, gun emplacements and cabin sites are visible. The site straddles the Parkersburg and Staunton Turnpike and was a campground for Confederate troops in the winter of 1861-62. In elevation (4,250 feet) it was the highest Confederate winter campground of the war. Union Gen. Robert Milroy marched through Camp Bartow and on Dec. 13 attacked the entrenched Confederates and was replused. He retreated to Randolph County. The Confederates held the area through April, 1862 and then abandoned the region for the rest of the war because of bad weather at the site.

Many other engagements took place during the year, among them skirmishes at Falling Waters, Berkeley County, on July 2, at Bolivar Heights, Jefferson County, on Oct. 16, at Guyandotte, Cabel County, on Nov. 10, and to Sutton, Braxton County, on Dec. 29. Romney, Hampshire County, changed hands several times during the year. It was to change hands 56 times during the war. The year ended with most of western Virginia controlled by the Union. Gen. Rosecrans commanded a region with 40,000 troops, with Cox in the Kanawha Valley, Milroy in the Cheat Mountain area and Kelley guarding the B and O Railroad. The Confederate force was not large enough to retake the area.

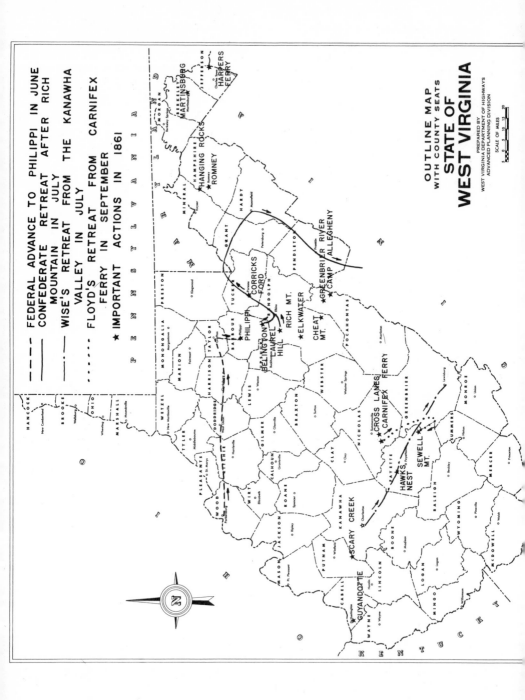

FEDERAL ADVANCE TO PHILIPPI IN JUNE
---- CONFEDERATE RETREAT AFTER RICH
         MOUNTAIN IN JULY
---- WISE'S RETREAT FROM THE KANAWHA
         VALLEY IN JULY
······ FLOYD'S RETREAT FROM CARNIFEX
         FERRY IN SEPTEMBER
★ IMPORTANT ACTIONS IN 1861

OUTLINE MAP
WITH COUNTY SEATS
STATE OF
WEST VIRGINIA

PREPARED BY
WEST VIRGINIA DEPARTMENT OF HIGHWAYS
ADVANCED PLANNING DIVISION

SCALE OF MILES

Union Volunteers assembled on High Street in 1861, in Morgantown, Monongalia County. Courtesy of WVU Library Archives.

Harpers Ferry, Jefferson County 1860. Courtesy Harpers Ferry National Historical Park.

Present day Harpers Ferry, Jefferson County from Maryland Heights. Courtesy of Harpers Ferry National Historical Park

Harpers Ferry in July 1861, showing damage after Confederates had withdrawn from the town. Courtesy Harpers Ferry National Historical Park.

Shenandoah Street, Harpers Ferry, Jefferson County.

31

General Jackson's Headquarters at Harpers Ferry, June 1861.

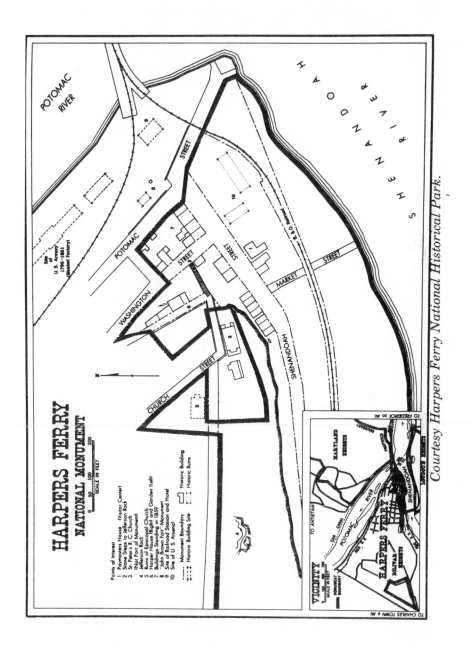

HARPERS FERRY
NATIONAL MONUMENT

0   50   100   200
SCALE IN FEET

POTOMAC RIVER

Site of U.S. Armory 1796-1861 (Musket Factory)

POTOMAC STREET

WASHINGTON STREET

CHURCH STREET

POTOMAC STREET

MARKET STREET

SHENANDOAH STREET

B & O. Railroad

SHENANDOAH RIVER

Points of Interest
1. Paymasters House (Visitor Center)
2. Stone Steps to Jefferson Rock
3. St. Peter's R. C. Church
   (Not Part of Monument)
4. Jefferson Rock
5. Ruins of Episcopal Church
6. Harper House (Right) and Garden (Left)
7. Buildings Standing in 1859
8. John Brown Fort Monument
9. Site of Railroad Station and Hotel
10. Site of U. S. Arsenal

☐ Historic Building
▨ Historic Ruins

— · — Monument Boundary
‡ · · · ‡ Historic Building Site

VICINITY
SCALE IN MILES

— Monument Boundary

TO ANTIETAM

C&O CANAL

POTOMAC RIVER

MARYLAND HEIGHTS

TO FREDERICK 20 MI.

HARPERS FERRY

BOLIVAR HEIGHTS

SHENANDOAH RIVER

LOUDOUN HEIGHTS

TO CHARLES TOWN 6 MI.

SHENANDOAH RIVER

Courtesy Harpers Ferry National Historical Park.

Map 3

33

Landing of Federal troops at Parkersburg 1861.

Monument to Thornsberry Bailey Brown at Grafton, Taylor County on Route 50 at Tygart Valley River bridge. Brown was the first Union soldier killed in the war on May 22, 1861.

Sycamore Dale near Romney, Hampshire County on Route 28. Headquarters of Union General Lew Wallace, author of "Ben Hur," in 1861. McNeill's Rangers surrendered here in April 1865.

36

Original Baltimore and Ohio Railroad hotel at Martinsburg, Berkeley County. Across from the roundhouse.

The Baltimore and Ohio Railroad Roundhouse in Martinsburg, Berkeley County. From Civil War Railroads by Geo. G. Abdill.

38

Baltimore and Ohio Railroad Roundhouse at Martinsburg, Berkeley County. Part of this structure survived burning of railroad facilities by General Jackson on June 20, 1861.

THE FIGHT AT PHILIPPI, VA., JUNE 3D, 1861.—THE UNITED STATES TROOPS UNDER COMMAND OF COLONEL DUMONT, SUPPORTED BY COLONELS KELLEY AND LANDER; THE CONFEDERATES, UNDER COLONEL PORTERFIELD.

Battle of Philippi, Barbour County, June 3, 1861. First land battle of the Civil War.

College Hill at Alderson-Broaddus College, Philippi. Site of Union cannon that fired the first shot of the battle.

Philippi Bridge on Route 250 over Tygart Valley River through which both armies passed during the war. Used as a barracks for Union troops. It was thought to have been mined during the war in case southern troops threatened it. Built in 1852

General Rosecrans and staff at his headquarters at Clarksburg, Harrison County in 1861. Courtesy W. Va. Hillbilly.

43

THE ENGAGEMENT AT BEALINGTON, VA., BETWEEN OHIO AND INDIANA REGIMENTS AND A DETACHMENT OF GEORGIA TROOPS.
From a Sketch by H. Lovie.

Battle of Belington, Barbour County July 8, 1861.

44

View of Belington, Barbour County from Laurel Hill. Site of Confederate fortified position. June 16-July 12, 1861. Arrow points to Camp Laurel campground.

THE BATTLE OF RICH MOUNTAIN, VA.—THE UNITED STATES TROOPS UNDER GENERAL ROSECRANS, OF GENERAL McCLELLAN'S COMMAND; THE CONFEDERATES UNDER GENERAL PEGRAM.—THE THIRTEENTH INDIANA CAPTURE A GUN.

Battle of Rich Mountain July 11, 1861.

46

Rich Mountain Battlefield site, five miles west of Beverly, Randolph County on Route 219. Battle fought July 11, 1861 in these woods. Some of the rocks have names of the soldiers carved on them.

47

Rich Mountain Battlefield site from Union side looking north. July, 1884. Showing Hart house and barn. Battle fought around these buildings. Courtesy of WVU Library Archives.

Rich Mountain Battlefield site looking at barn site.

49

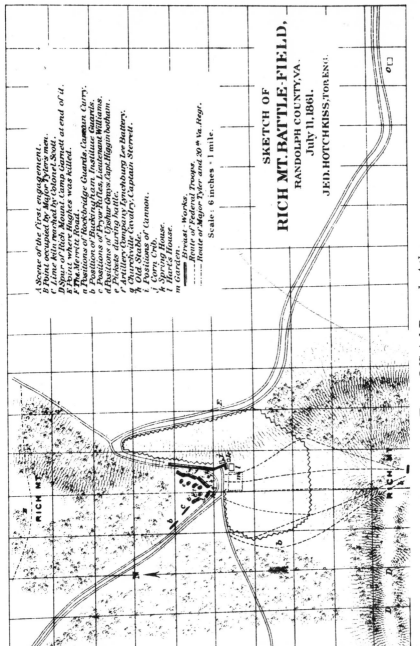

SKETCH OF
RICH MT. BATTLE-FIELD,
RANDOLPH COUNTY, VA.
July 11, 1861.

JED. HOTCHKISS, TOP. ENG.

Scale: 6 inches = 1 mile.

A *Scene of the first engagement.*
B *Point occupied by Major Tyler's men.*
C *Lime kiln reached by Colonel Scott.*
D *Spur of Rich Mount. Camp Garnett at end of it.*
E *Point where Hughes was killed.*
F *The Merritt Road.*
a *Positions of Rockbridge Guards, Captain Curry.*
b *Position of Buckingham Institute Guards.*
c *Positions of Pryor Rifles, Lieutenant Williams.*
d *Positions of Upshur Grays, Capt. Higginbotham.*
e *Pickets during battle.*
f *Artillery Company Lynchburg Lee Battery.*
g *Churchville Cavalry, Captain Sterrett.*
h *Old Stable.*
i *Positions of Cannon.*
j *Corn Crib.*
k *Spring House.*
l *Hart's House.*
m *Garden.*

━━━ *Breast-Works.*
──── *Route of Federal Troops.*
- - - - *Route of Major Tyler and 20ᵗʰ Va.Regt.*

From Official Records-Atlas.

50

Colonel Steedman's Fourteenth Ohio Regiment on the Bank of the Cheat River.   General Garnett's Position on the Cliff.   Dumont's Men Crossing the River and Climbing the Cliff to Turn the Enemy's Position.

THE BATTLE AT CARRICK'S FORD, VA., BETWEEN THE TROOPS OF GENERAL McCLELLAN'S COMMAND, LED BY GENERAL MORRIS, AND THE CONFEDERATE ARMY, UNDER GENERAL GARNETT, JULY 13TH. 1861.

Battle of Corricks Ford July 13, 1861.

Corricks Ford Battle site, Parsons, Tucker County on Route 219. General Garnett was killed here July 13, 1861.

Drawing of Cheat Mountain Summit Fort near Cheat Bridge in Randolph County just off Route 219. Built by Union Army in 1861. Drawn by a soldier in the 2nd W. Va. Infantry.

Cheat Mountain Summit Fort looking east. Arrows point to fort outline.

Cheat Mountain Summit Fort. Arrows show breastwork remains.

Busrod-Crawford House, Beverly on Route 219. Site of General McClellan's telegraph station. First use of telegraph in warfare.

James Logan House, Beverly on Route 219. Scene of the first amputation on a Union soldier in the war in July 1861.

David Goff House, Beverly on Route 219. Used as a hospital during the war.

Monument erected in memory of Lt. Col. John A. Washington C.S.A., south of Elkwater, Randolph County on Route 219. Aide-de-camp to General Lee, killed September 13, 1861 at Elkwater.

Monument at Valley Mountain Campsite of General Lee's Command in 1861. Near Mace, Pocahontas County. Courtesy of Jack Zinn, Nutter Fort, W. Va.

Valley Mountain Campsite of General Lee's Command in 1861. Near Mace, Pocahontas County. Courtesy of Jack Zinn, Nutter Fort, W. Va.

Site of Lee Tree on top of Sewell Mountain, Fayette County on Route 60. Tree stood until 1937. General Lee camped here in September, 1861 and bought his horse Traveller here.

Busters Knob opposite Sewell Mountain, Fayette County on Route 60. Fortified position during Lee's campaign in 1861.

Dietz Farm at Meadow Bluff in Greenbrier County near Sam Black Church off Route 60. Campsite of both armies during the war. House was Lee's headquarters in 1861 and used as a hospital.

Site of Battle of Scary Creek on Route 35 in Putnam County. Battle took place July 17, 1861.

Morgan's Kitchen Museum at St. Albans, Kanawha County on Route 60. Built in 1846 and originally at Morgan's farm near Scary Creek. Union troops were fed from this kitchen the day before the Battle of Scary Creek.

Site of Battle of Cross Lanes on Route 129 in Nicholas County, at Kesslers Cross Lanes. Battle fought on August 26, 1861.

Union headquarters at Kesslers Cross Lanes on Route 129 in Nicholas County.

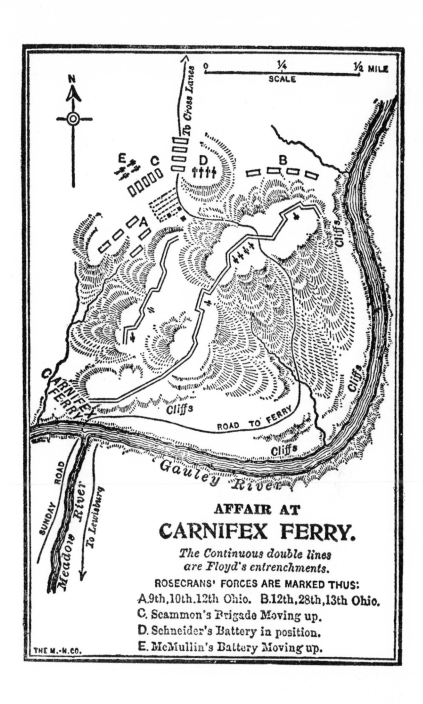

AFFAIR AT
CARNIFEX FERRY.

*The Continuous double lines
are Floyd's entrenchments.*

ROSECRANS' FORCES ARE MARKED THUS:

A. 9th, 10th, 12th Ohio. **B.** 12th, 28th, 13th Ohio.
C. Scammon's Brigade Moving up.
D. Schneider's Battery in position.
E. McMullin's Battery Moving up.

From Official Records-Atlas.

Map 4

Copy of drawing by J. Nep. Roesler Corporal of Color Guard, Company G, 47th Regiment, Ohio Volunteers, US Army. Drawing done on stone.

70

Patteson House at Carnifex Ferry Battlefield State Park just off Route 129 in Nicholas County. Scene of battle September 10, 1861. House was used as a Federal hospital and has been completely rebuilt by the state.

Foxhole on Patteson Trail, Carnifex Ferry Battlefield State Park. Part of the battle took place in these woods September 10, 1861.

Travelers' Repose at Bartow, Pocahontas County on Routes 250 and 92. Built before the war as an Inn on the Parkersburg and Staunton Turnpike. Scene of the Battle of Greenbrier River October 3, 1861.

Camp Bartow, Bartow, Pocahontas County. Constructed by Confederate Army in 1861 to guard the Parkersburg and Staunton Turnpike. Scene of battle October 3, 1861.

Camp Bartow at Bartow, Pocahontas County. Gun emplacement looking west.

Top of Allegheny Fort and Campground site, Pocahontas County, just off Route 250, near Virginia border. Showing trenches and chimney piles (arrow) left from huts built by Confederate soldiers, winter of 1861-62. Scene of battle December 13, 1861.

Top of Allegheny, gun enplacement in middle of fort.

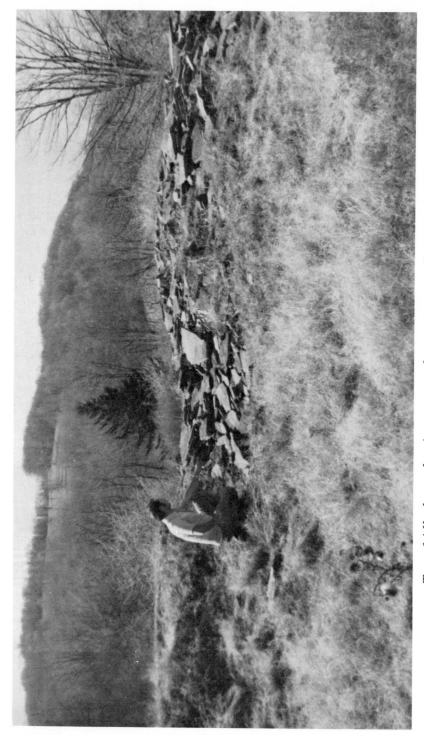

Top of Allegheny showing gun emplacement on southwest end of fort.

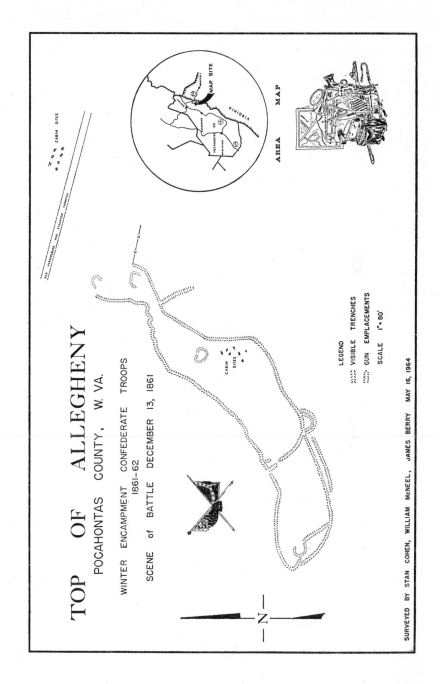

TOP OF ALLEGHENY

POCAHONTAS COUNTY, W. VA.

WINTER ENCAMPMENT CONFEDERATE TROOPS
1861-62

SCENE of BATTLE DECEMBER 13, 1861

LEGEND

VISIBLE TRENCHES

GUN EMPLACEMENTS

SCALE 1" = 80'

SURVEYED BY STAN COHEN, WILLIAM McNEEL, JAMES BERRY MAY 16, 1964

CABIN SITES

OLD PARKERSBURG AND STAUNTON TURNPIKE

CABIN SITES

MAP SITE

VIRGINIA

POCAHONTAS CO

AREA MAP

N

Map 5

79

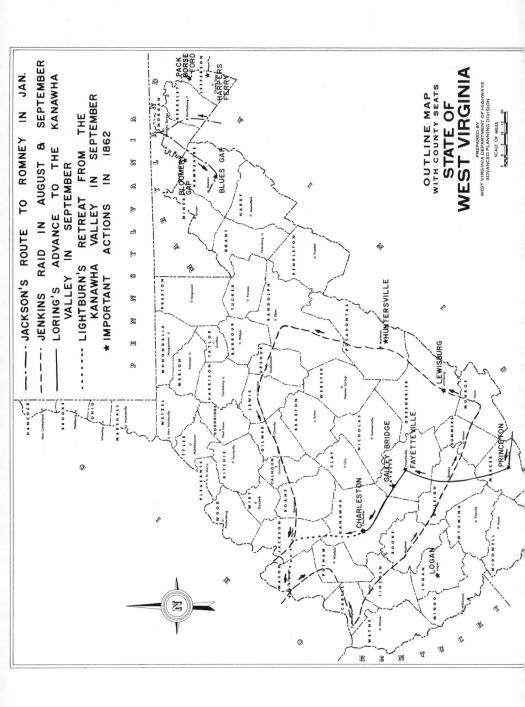

Map 6

1862
CONSOLIDATION

JACKSON'S CAMPAIGN

Stonewall Jackson was placed in command of the Valley District in late 1861 with headquarters in Winchester, Virginia. He wanted to clear the Federals from the district and destroy the B and O Railroad, and his first object was to capture Romney, Hampshire County. He left Winchester Jan. 1, 1862, marching first to Berkeley Springs, Morgan County and then to Hancock, Maryland, but he could not take Hancock and his troops were turned back at Blues Gap, fifteen miles east of Romney. The Union commander, thinking Jackson had an overwhelming superiority of number, evacuated Romney, however, and Jackson moved in.

Jackson considered Romney a strategic base and ordered Gen. Loring to hold the town while he returned to Winchester. There was a lot of resentment against Jackson for keeping Loring at Romney and he was accused of committing a strategic blunder. Letters were written to the Confederate secretary of war in Richmond complaining of conditions in Romney, and on Jan. 30 Loring was directed to evacuate the town in defiance of Jackson's authority. Jackson reluctantly ordered Loring back to Winchester and then wrote a letter of resignation from the army. Governor Letcher and Gen. Joseph Johnston persuaded him to withdraw his letter for the good of the Confederacy. Loring was transferred to southwest Virginia and Jackson went on to immortality.

BURNING OF PRINCETON

Princeton was the county seat of Mercer County in 1862 and was one of the few towns with southern sympathies burned by the Confederates during the war. It was set afire on May 1 to keep the supplies stored there from falling into Union hands, but a Federal force under Col. Rutherford B. Hayes saved part of the town. (Lt. William McKinley served under Hayes there.) The Boone and Logan County courthouses had been burned earlier by Federal troops.

BATTLE OF LEWISBURG

One of the most strategic towns in West Virginia was Lewisburg, Greenbrier County. It straddled the James River and Kanawha Turnpike and was the gateway to the Kanawha Valley and the Virginia Valley.

Col. George Crook, commanding Union troops, had been on a railroad raid near Covington, Virginia, when he learned that Gen. Henry Heth's southern troops were hurring toward him. He proceeded to Lewisburg and occupied the town on May 12. Heth attacked the town on the morning of May 23 and caught the Federal troops by surprise. However, after reforming their lines, the Federals beat back the Confederates who retreated to Caldwell, a few miles west of Lewisburg, burned the covered bridge spanning the Greenbrier River, and then fled down to Monroe County.

A Revolutionary War cannon used by the Confederates was captured during the battle. It had first been captured at Yorktown in 1781 and was pressed into service again in 1861. It was sent to Springfield, Ohio, the hometown of one of the Union regiments that fought in the battle, and was placed in front of the Memorial Hall there.

JENKINS RAID

Gen. Albert G. Jenkins of Cabell County led a raiding party of 550 Confederate cavalrymen from Salt Sulphur Springs in Monroe County on Aug. 24. He passed through Greenbrier, Pocahontas and Randolph Counties and after capturing the towns of Buckhannon, Weston, Glenville, Spencer and Ripley, crossed into Ohio, becoming the first commander to carry the Confederate flag into that state. He recrossed into West Virginia below Point Pleasant, Mason County, and marched to Guyandotte and Raleigh Courthouse. His raid dramatized the inadequacy of Union defenses, weakened early in August by the transfer of 5,000 troops from the Kanawha Valley command to Gen. John Pope's army in Virginia. This raid convinced the Confederate command that they could retake the Kanawha Valley, and Gen. Loring did so in September.

HARPERS FERRY

Lee's invasion of Maryland through the eastern panhandle in September caused much excitement in that part of the state. Lee's army crossed the Potomac at a ford east of Shepherdstown, Jefferson County, on Sept. 16 on its way to the Battle of Antietam. Stonewall Jackson split off from the main army and surrounded Harpers Ferry. Gen. Lafayette McLaws occupied Maryland Heights and Gen. Walker Loudoun Heights, and the School House Hill was lined with artillery. Gen. A.P. Hill was in direct command, and after a two-day seige forced Col. Dixon Miles to surrender his 11,000 troops, 13,000 small arms and 73 artillery pieces. Jackson left Hill with the prisoners and marched his troops to help Lee at Antietam. The battle was actually a draw, but it stopped Lee from making his first invasion of northern territory. His army recrossed the Potomac near Shepherdstown into West Virginia on Sept. 18, but Gen. McClellan did not pursue him far.

President Lincoln visited Harpers Ferry in October to view the town and try to get Gen. McClellan moving again against Lee. He viewed the area but could not budge McClellan.

KANAWHA VALLEY CAMPAIGN

In 1862 Union forces controlled the Kanawha Valley with a large supply depot at Gauley Bridge and forts at Fayetteville and other points. Gen. Joseph A.J. Lightburn from Lewis County was in command although some of his troops had been transferred to Virginia. Gen. Loring, the Confederate commander, was stationed at Pearisburg, Virginia, and Lee directed him to again invade the area, capture the Kanawha Valley and use it as a base to recover Trans-Allegheny Virginia. The salt supply at Charleston was a deciding factor in this operation, as the south was short of salt.

Loring left Sept. 1 with 4,000 troops and marched to Fayetteville. A battle there on Sept. 11 resulted in an unexpected Union rout. Lightburn ordered a general retreat and called in his outposts at Ansted and Summersville, thus opening up the entire Kanawha Valley. He retreated down the Cotton Hill road near Gauley Bridge to Marmet in Kanawha County while the main body of his troops retreated down the Kanawha Turnpike with a wagon train thirteen miles long. His army finally rejoined at Charleston for defense of the city.

A second bridge across Gauley River at Gauley Bridge, Fayette County, was again destroyed, this time by the Union forces on their retreat. The first bridge had been destroyed during Wise's retreat from the Valley in July, 1861. The Confederates had pulled a brass cannon up on Cotton Hill overlooking Gauley Bridge to bombard the town. Upon seeing the Federals retreating, the Southerners threw the cannon over the hill and abandoned it in their haste to capture the supplies in the town. Several expeditions in recent years attempted to locate this cannon without success, and it may still be there in the woods.

Early in the morning of Sept. 13, the first units of Loring's army arrived in Charleston in the vicinity of the present Morris Harvy College. After an all day battle Lightburn retreated toward the Ohio River, cutting the cables on the bridge over the Elk River at Charleston. Loring did not pursue him. The southern forces came into the Kanawha Valley not as invaders but as liberators and Loring issued this proclamation:

To the People of Western Virginia.

The Army of the Confederate States has come among you to expel the enemy, to rescue the people from the despotism of the counterfeit State Government imposed upon you by Northern bayonets, and to restore the country once more to its natural allegiance to the State. We fight for peace and the possession of our own territory. We do not intend to punish those who remain at home as quiet citizens in obedience to the laws of the land, and to all such clemency and amnesty are declared; but those who persist in adhering to the cause of the public enemy, and the pretended

84

State Government he has erected at Wheeling, will be dealt with as their obstinate treachery deserves.

When the liberal policy of the Confederate Government shall be introduced and made known to the people, who have so long experienced the wanton misrule of the invader, the Commanding General expects the people heartily to sustain it not only as a duty, but as a deliverance from their taskmasters and usurpers. Indeed, he already recognizes in the cordial welcome which the people everywhere give to the Army, a happy indication of their attachment to their true and lawful Government.

Until the proper authorities shall order otherwise, and in the absence of municipal law and its customary ministers, Marital Law will be administered by the Army and the Provost Marshals. Private rights and property will be respected, violence will be repressed, and order promoted, and all the private property used by the Army will be paid for.

The Commanding General appeals to all good citizens to aid him in these objects, and to all able-bodied men to join his army to defend the sanctities of religion and virtue, home, territory, honor, and law, which are invaded and violated by an unscrupulous enemy, whom an indignant and united people are now about to chastise on his own soil.

The Government expects an immediate and enthusiastic response to this call. Your country has been reclaimed for you from the enemy by soldiers, many of whom are from distant parts of the State, and the Confederacy; and you will prove unworthy to possess so beautiful and fruitful a land, if you do not now rise to retain and defend it. The oaths which the invader imposed upon you are void. They are immoral attempts to restrain you from your duty to your State and Government. They do not exempt you from the obligation to support your Government and to serve in the Army; and if such persons are taken as prisoners of war, the Confederate Government guarantees to them the humane treatment of the usages of war.

> By command of
> MAJ. GEN. LORING
> H. Fitzhugh
> Chief of Staff

The Confederate occupation did not last long. Concentrations of Federal troops at Clarksburg and Point Pleasant forced Loring to abandon the valley and retreat toward Lewisburg on Oct. 8

after originally being ordered to march on the Cheat River Bridge in Preston County. He was relieved of his command on Oct. 16 and Gen. John Echols of Monroe County took over and moved back into Charleston. He was in turn forced out of the valley Oct. 29, and the valley was in Northern hands for good. During most of the six-week occupation the Confederates concentrated on moving salt out of Kanawha Salines to eastern Virginia.

CAMP, GAULEY BRIDGE.

Printed by Ehrgott, Forbriger & Co. Cincinnati.

Copy of drawing by J. Nep. Roesler Corporal of Color Guard, Company G, 47th Regiment, Ohio Volunteers, US Army. Drawing done on stone in 1861. Courtesy W. Va. Dept. of Archives and History.

Copy of drawings by J. Nep. Roesler Corporal of Color Guard, Company G, 47th Regiment, Ohio Volunteers, US Army. Drawing done on stone in 1861. Courtesy W. Va. Dept. of Archives and History.

CROSSING TO FAYETTEVILLE.

Printed by Krappe, Forbrger & Co. Cincinnati.

Copy of drawing by J. Nep. Roesler Corporal of Color Guard, Company G, 47th Regiment, Ohio Volunteers, US Army. Drawing done on stone in 1861. Courtesy W. Va. Dept. of Archives and History.

Old Stone Church in Lewisburg, Greenbrier County. Built in 1796 and used as a hospital and barracks during the war. Courtesy of the W. Va. Dept. of Commerce.

Greenbrier County Library and Muesum in Lewisburg. Built in 1834 to house the law library of the Virginia Supreme Court of Appeals. Used as a hospital during the war.

Frazer's Inn (The Star Tavern) in Lewisburg. Built in 1820 and used as a residence for lawyers attending court. More recently owned by the Greenbrier College for Women.

Original building of the Lewisburg Academy built about 1812. Used as a hospital and barracks during the war.

Greenbrier County Courthouse, Lewisburg. Built in 1837.

John Wesley Methodist Church, Lewisburg. Built in 1820. Cannon fire struck building during Lewisburg Battle, May 23, 1862.

Valley View Farm on Route 60, two miles west of Lewisburg. Formerly known as Tuckwiller's Tavern. Built in 1828. Skirmish near here on May 2, 1863 resulting in a Union defeat. House used as a hospital and headquarters for Union troops.

Elmhurst at Caldwell, Greenbrier County on Route 60. Built in 1824 and used as a stage stop. Skirmish fought here after Battle of Lewisburg in May 1862.

Pack Horse Ford across Potomac River east of Shepherdstown, Jefferson County. Used by both armies during the war. Scene of crossing by General Lee's Army at the Battle of Antietam September 1862.

Ford near Shepherdstown. Union soldiers firing across Potomac, late September, 1862. Drawing by Alfred R. Waud. Courtesy of W. Va. Dept. of Archives & History.

Fort Scammon on top of Fort Hill in Charleston, Kanawha County. Built by Union troops to protect Charleston. Breastworks still plainly visible.

CHARLESTON
Sept. 13ᵗʰ 1862 . 34ᵗʰ, 37ᵗʰ, 44ᵗʰ, & 47ᵗʰ, O V I

At the height of the "Battle of Charleston," federal soldiers cut cables on the suspension bridge across Elk River.

Lightburn's troops cutting the cables of the Elk River Bridge at Charleston, Kanawha County on their retreat from the city in September, 1862.

101

GENERAL ORDER.

HEAD QUARTERS,
DEPARTMENT OF WESTERN VIRGINIA,
Charleston, Va., Sept. 24, 1862.

General Order, No.

The money issued by the Confederate Government is secure, and is receivable in payment of public dues, and convertible into 8 per cent. bonds. Citizens owe it to the country to receive it in trade; and it will therefore be regarded as good in payment for supplies purchased for the army.

Persons engaged in trade are invited to resume their business and open their stores.

By order of

MAJ. GEN. LORING.

General order issued by General Loring upon his capture of Charleston, Kanawha County in September, 1862. Courtesy of W. Va. Dept. of Archives and History.

THE GUERILLA.

DEVOTED TO SOUTHERN RIGHTS AND INSTITUTIONS.

Vol. 1.   CHARLESTON, VA., OCTOBER 3, 1862.   No. 6

THE GUERILLA,

IS PUBLISHED EVERY AFTERNOON

By the Associate Printers.

TERMS—TEN CENTS per copy, or FIFTY CENTS per week.

Rates of Advertising.

One square, (10 lines,) first insertion 50 cents.
Each subsequent insertion, - - - - 25 "
Advertisers will please mark the number of insertions wanted on the MS., or they will be continued until ordered out, and charged accordingly.

FOR THE GUERILLA.

TO ****.

I THINK OF THEE.

I.

I think of thee when twilight shade
Hath spread its mantle o'er the day,
To hide the sunbeams from our view,
And clothe the earth in silver grey.
I think of all thy virtues sare—
Thy beauty, grace and winning ways,
And humbly breathe a fervent prayer
That God may bless thee all thy days.

II.

I think of thee, when Luna sheds
Her mystic light down from above;
And basking 'neath her mellow beams,
I realize the heart's first love.
And then when thoughts recall the past—
The joyous scenes of other years—
I sigh because I knew thee not,
Till sighing fills my eyes with tears.

III.

I think of thee at midnight hour,
When all on earth is hushed to rest,
And try to drive away the care
That dwells within my troubled breast.
And when in sleep I seek repose,
And strive to ease my aching heart,
Some idle dream will bring thee close,
And make my restless spirit start!

IV.

I think of thee when morning's light
Bids the darkness disappear;
And in dreamy visions bright
I see thy gentle spirit near.
I think of no one else but thee,
For no one else is half so dear;
Then if in battle I should fall!
Shed for me a single tear.
" WILTON."
Camp near Charleston, Oct. 1st, 1862.

A TALE OF TERROR.

At the "Crow Inn," at Antwerp, some years ago, a white spectre was seen bearing a lamp in one hand, and a bunch of keys in the other—this unpleasant visitor was seen by a variety of travelers, passing along a corridor.

Nothing would satisfy the neighbors that an unfortunate traveler had not been, at some period or other, despatched in that fatal room by one of the previous landlords of the house; and the hotel gradually obtained the name of the "Haunted Inn," and ceased to be frequented by its old patrons.

The landlord finding himself on the brink of ruin, determined to sleep in the haunted room, with a view of proving the groundlessness of the story. To make the matter more sure, as he said, he caused a hustler to bear him company, on pretence of requiring a witness to the absurdity of the report; but, in reality, from cowardice. At dead of night, however, just as the two men were composing themselves to sleep in one bed—leaving another which was in the room untenanted—the door flew open, and in glided the white spectre!

Without pausing to ascertain what it might attempt on approaching the other bed, towards which it directed its course, the two men rushed naked out of the room, and by the alarm they created, confirmed more fully than ever the evil repute of the house.

Unable longer to sustain the cost of so unproductive an establishment, the poor landlord advertised for sale the house in which he and his father before him were born and had passed their lives. But bidders were as scarce as customers; the inn remained on sale for nearly a year, during which, from time to time, the spectre reappeared.

At length an officer of the garrison, who had formerly frequented the house, and recollected the excellent quality of its wine, moved to compassion in favor of the poor host, undertook to clear up the mystery by sleeping in the aforesaid haunted chamber; nothing doubting that the whole was a trick of some envious neighbor, desirous of deteriorating the value of the freehold in order to become a purchaser.

His offer having been gratefully accepted, the captain took up his quarters in the fatal room, with a bottle of wine, and a brace of loaded pistols on the table before him; determined to fire at whatever object might enter the doors.

At the usual hour of midnight, accordingly, when the door flew open and the white spectre, bearing a lamp and a bunch of keys, made its appearance, he seized both his pistols, when, fortunately, as his finger was on the point of touching the trigger, he perceived that the apparition was no other than the daughter of his host, a young and pretty girl, evidently walking in her sleep. Preserving the strictest silence, he watched her set down the lamp, place her keys carefully on the chimney place, and retire to the opposite bed, which, as it afterwards proved, she had often occupied during the lifetime of her late mother, who slept in the room.

No sooner had she thoroughly composed herself, than the officer, after locking the door of the room, went in search of her father and several competent witnesses, including the water bailiff of the district, who had been the loudest in circulating rumors concerning the Haunted Inn. The poor girl was found quietly asleep in bed, and her terror on awaking in the dreaded chamber afforded sufficient evidence to all present of the state of somnambulism in which she had been entranced.

From that period the spectre was seen no more; partly because the landlord's daughter shortly after removed to a home of her own; and the tales of horror so freely circulated to the bewilderment of the poor neighbors, ended in the simple story of a young girl walking in her sleep.

ALWAYS BE PREPARED FOR DEATH.—This was the admonition of a Missouri elder, as he placed in his son's belt two bowie-knives and a pair of revolvers.

TO KILL MOSQUITOES.—Chain their hind legs to a tree, then go round in front and make faces at them.

A SPLENDID CHANCE.

A FLYING BATTERY is about to be formed for *Gen. Jenkins' Cavalry Brigade*, to be officered by experienced artillerists, and to be equipped in the most superb style. The Battery is to consist of two three-inch rifled guns, two twelve pound howitzers, (light, such as the Richmond Howitzer Battalion has,) and two mountain rifled guns, to be packed, when necessary, on horses.—Fleet, active horses for the pieces are now being purchased by the Quartermaster of Jenkins' Brigade, and all necessary steps for the procurement of a complete outfit are being taken. Applicants for membership will be required to undergo a medical examination, and must be *young, active and intelligent*. The cannoneers will be mounted, and must furnish their own horses, which will be valued and paid for.

While it is expected to recruit the men from among the mounted companies now forming in this section, transfers can doubtless be procured for a few enterprising men from the regiments and battalions.

The service is a brilliant one, full of exciting incident. *No half-asleep men need apply!* A Recruiting Sergeant may be found for the present at the ORDNANCE OFFICE in Charleston.

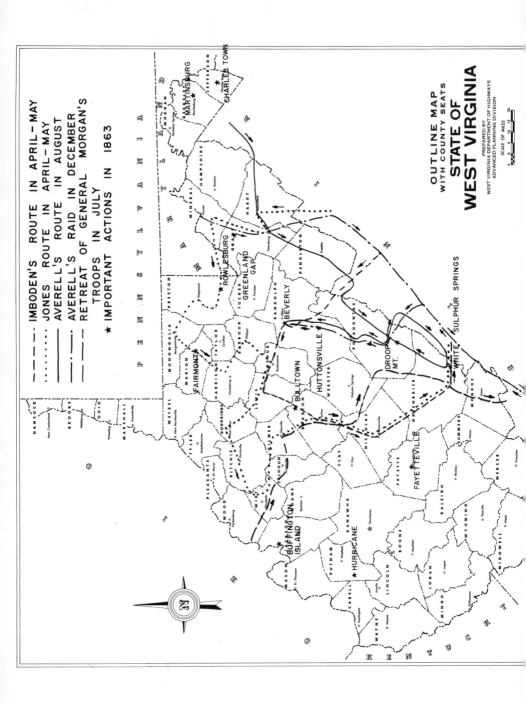

OUTLINE MAP
WITH COUNTY SEATS
STATE OF
WEST VIRGINIA

PREPARED BY
WEST VIRGINIA DEPARTMENT OF HIGHWAYS
ADVANCED PLANNING DIVISION

SCALE OF MILES

IMBODEN'S ROUTE IN APRIL-MAY

JONES' ROUTE IN APRIL-MAY

AVERELL'S ROUTE IN AUGUST

AVERELL'S RAID IN DECEMBER

RETREAT OF GENERAL MORGAN'S
          TROOPS IN JULY

★ IMPORTANT ACTIONS IN 1863

Map 7

104

1863
The Year of the Raids

Confederate armies were riding high at the beginning of 1863 in the eastern and western theaters of war, and their successes were to continue until the twin disasters of Vicksburg and Gettysburg in July. However, in West Virginia, the Union forces had consolidated their positions and the destruction of the Virginia and Tennessee Railroad in Virginia became one of their major objectives. The Confederates had to be content with making raids to obtain supplies and disrupt the B and O Railroad.

JONES-IMBODEN RAID

Gen. Lee wrote to Gen. John D. Imboden outlining a policy of war for West Virginia and urged him to carry it out. Among other things, the municipal officers of the Reorganized Government of Virginia, called by Lee "the Pierpont government," were to be captured whenever possible, and Imboden was instructed to "render the position of sheriff as dangerous a position as possible."

The great raid of the year was conducted by Confederate Gens. Imboden and William E. Jones. Jones was the ranking officer but the plan was formulated by Imboden. He wrote Gen. Lee outlining plans for a raid to destroy the B and O Railroad from Oakland, Maryland, to Grafton; defeat the enemy at Beverly, Philippi and Buckhannon; recruit for the Confederate army and control the northwest part of the state to enable the people to take part in the Virginia state elections in May. Except for the partial destruction of the railroad and the capture of thousands of horses and cattle, the raid was of little benefit to the Confederacy.

Lee split the raiders into two independent groups commanded by Jones and Imboden, but the forces were to join later. Imboden left Shenandoah Mountain near Staunton, Virginia, with 3,400 infantry on April 20, 1863. He marched to Beverly and then to Buckhannon, Upsher County, which he occupied April 29 and waited for Jones to meet him. His main objectives were Grafton and Clarksburg, but they were too strongly defended to be attacked.

Jones left Lacey Springs, Virginia, on April 21 with 1,300 men. He marched through Moorefield and Petersburg and fought a battle at Greenland Gap in Grant County. On April 26 he attacked Rowlesburg in Preston County in a bid to destroy the B and O Railroad trestles across Cheat River. He could not accomplish this and thus one of the main objectives of the raid was not carried out. His troops marched to Morgantown, Monongalia County, took the town and then proceeded to Fairmont, Marion County, where they destroyed the large iron railroad bridge across the Monongahela River. He bypassed Clarksburg and Grafton, marched to Philippi and found Imboden at Buckhannon. They planned to capture Clarksburg, a large Federal supply depot, and moved to Weston, Lewis County for the attack. But Clarksburg was still too strongly defended, so Imboden moved on to Summersville, Nicholas County.

Jones left Weston on May 6 and passed through West Union and Cario via the Parkersburg pike in an effort to cut the Northwestern Virginia Railroad. On May 9 he swung toward "Oiltown" (Burning Springs in Wirt County) and his troops went up the hollows and ravines and put the torch to oil storage tanks and loaded barges on the Little Kanawha River and Burning Springs Run. The whole countryside was ablaze and 150,000 barrels of oil went up in smoke. This was the first burning of an oil installation in the history of warfare.

The two separate forces were united at Summersville on May 14 and made their way back to the security of the Confederate lines in the Shenandoah Valley.

INDIRECT ARTILLERY FIRE

Indirect artillery fire was used for the first time in modern warfare at Fayetteville, Fayette County, on May 19, 1863, by Sgt.

Milton Humphreys and a Confederate artillery battery firing on Fort Scammon. Humphreys placed his battery behind a clump of trees and arched his shells over a hill into the fort. He stationed an observer on a hill to direct the fire. He dropped 69 shells into the fort and the Union troops thought they came from the sky.

BEVERLY RAID

On July 3 Confederate Gen. William L. Jackson and 1,200 men raided Beverly. He entered Randolph County by way of Valley Head and Cheat Mountain and attacked from three directions. One of the three columns found a still along the way and stopped to sample the brew, thus delaying the attack. Union Gen. William W. Averell marched over from Philippi and the Southerners retreated.

SOUTHERN SYMPATHIES

Illustrative of the divided loyalties of the people of the state is this order of assessment placed on Southern sympathizers by Union forces in Tucker County to compensate Union sympathizers for theft and destruction of property. This was directed to an Adam Harper:

St. George, Tucker County, Va. 11/28/62

Mr. Adam Harper, Sir:

In consequence of certain roberies which have been committed upon citizens of this country by bands of Gurilies you are hereby assessed to the amount of (285.00) Two Hundred and 85 Dollars to make good their losses. And upon your failure to make good this assessment by the 8th day of Dec., the following order has been issued to me by Brigadier General R.H. Milroy:

"You are to burn their houses, sieze their property and shoot them. You will be sure that you strictly carry out this order. You will require of the inhabitants for ten or fifteen miles around your camp on all the roads approaching the town upon which the enemy may approach that they must dash in and give you notice and that upon any one failing to do so you will burn their houses and shoot the men.

By order of
Brig. Gen. R.H. Milroy
Captain Kellogg Commanding 123rd Ohio

This assessment was disliked by both sides and Milroy's superiors put a stop to the practice soon afterwards.

BATTLE OF WHITE SULPHUR SPRINGS

White Sulphur Springs is the site of a famous health spa and was the scene of a battle on Aug. 26 between 1,300 Union troops commanded by Gen. Averell and 2,000 Confederate troops under Col. Patton. Averell was directed to seize the law books at the Virginia State Law Library at Lewisburg, Greenbrier County, which were housed there for the convenience of the judges and lawyers at the Virginia Supreme Court of Appeals.

Averell left Winchester, Virginia, Aug. 5 and destroyed the saltpeter works at Franklin, Pendleton County. He marched to Warm Springs, Virginia, and then turned west toward Lewisburg on the James River Pike. The Confederates had marched down Anthony's Creek Road to intercept the Union force and the two armies met where the two roads intersected. The battle lasted all day and into the next. Both sides were running low on ammunition and Averell was forced to retreat when his gave out. He returned to Beverly by way of Huntersville and Marlinton in Pocahontas County. Casualties were high on both sides, and among the dead was Capt. Paul VonKoenig, a German baron who was serving as aide-de-camp to Averell. Some say he was shot by his own troops. The wounded on both sides were cared for at the health spa hotel in White Sulphur Springs.

BATTLE OF BULLTOWN

Bulltown in Braxton County was the scene of a battle on Oct. 13, and the Union victory helped maintain Northern control in central West Virginia. A fort was constructed on the important Weston-Gauley Bridge Pike. The Confederates attacked and demanded that the enemy surrender. The Union commander sent back a challenge to "come and take us." A second surrender ultimatium was given and the commander said he would "fight until hell froze over," and if he had to retreat, he would "retreat on the ice." The Confederates finally broke off the engagement and withdrew.

GENERAL MORGAN'S RAID

One of the most bizarre raids of the year was Confederate Gen. John Morgan's strike across Indiana and Ohio and into West Virginia in July. He had been ordered into Kentucky to repel a Union invasion but disobeyed orders. As he rode through the Indiana and Ohio countryside with his 2400 troops, he burned railroads and military supplies and threw the population into panic. The West Virginia Legislature was in session in Wheeling and it ajourned to form a military company of mainly older men to fight the expected invader.

Morgan arrived at Buffington's Island opposite Ravenswood, Jackson County, on July 18. His troops had traveled sixteen days and they were sick and worn out. The river had risen several feet and they could not cross against enemy opposition. Federal troops came from as far away as Fayette County to capture him. Two Union gunboats in West Virginia waters fired on the Confederate troops and forced Morgan up the Ohio River opposite Bellville, Wood County, where some of the men swam to the West Virginia shore. Morgan finally surrendered at Salineville, near East Liverpool, Ohio, on July 26. Some of his men retreated across West Virginia to safety in Virginia on one of the longest retreats of the war. The Buffington's Island battle was the only battle fought in Ohio during the war.

CHARLES TOWN ATTACK

Gen. Imboden's infantry marched 48 miles in one day to attack Charles Town, Jefferson County, on Oct. 18. He captured more than 400 Union troops and then retreated. He beat Napoleon's record of marching 36 miles in one day to fight a battle.

BATTLE OF DROOP MOUNTAIN

One of the most important battles to take place in West Virginia, and the last large-scale battle fought in the state, took place at Droop Mountain in the southern part of Pocahontas County on Nov. 6. The Confederates were under Gen. John Echols of Monroe County and the Union force was led by Gen. Averell. It was brother against brother again, with many West Virginia troops on each side. Casualties were high on both sides.

The Confederates had control of the entire Greenbrier River Valley and the Union command wanted to clear them out and strike for the Virginia and Tennessee Railroad to the south. It was hoped this move would relieve the Union forces in Tennessee who had been defeated at the Battle of Chickamauga in September. Averell left Beverly and Gen. Alfred Duffie left Charleston in a pincer movement to clear the valley. Echols was stationed at Lewisburg but had troops scattered throughout the valley.

Because of delays of the two Union columns, Echols had time to concentrate what forces he could gather on top of Droop Mountain guarding the road south to Lewisburg. This site was to become the highest battle in elevation of the Civil War. Echols had only about 1,700 men to oppose Averell's 3,000 to 4,000 troops, but the terrain was in his favor. He did not fortify his position or protect his flanks, however, and these failures cost him the battle. The Federals turned the Confederate flank and forced them to retreat through Lewisburg into Virginia. Gen. Duffie tried to get to Lewisburg ahead of the retreating army to cut it off but was not successful.

Although the Southerners were beaten, they did keep their army intact and save the railroad from destruction. Ten days later the Confederates reoccupied many areas of the Greenbrier Valley.

GENERAL AVERELL'S SALEM RAID

Once again Gen. Averell was called upon to attack the Virginia and Tennessee Railroad, this time to relieve Gen. Ambrose Burnside who was besieged in Knoxville, Tennessee. The railroad was a vital link in the southern supply system to Tennessee. Averell left Keyser, Mineral County, on Dec. 8 and by taking back roads marched around several Confederate armies. He reached Salem, Virginia, on Dec. 16 and took the town by surprise. Many miles of railroad were destroyed and supplies were burned. On his retreat to safety in West Virginia he had to avoid more than 12,000 Confederate troops, cross many swollen rivers and survive freezing weather. He captured a dispatch and learned that only the road leading across the mountains into Pocahontas County was open. He eluded the enemy and finally reached safety, thus completing one of the most successful raids of the war by either side.

Site of Rathbone's oil well at Burning Springs, Wirt County on Route 5. Completed in 1860. Oil field facilities burned by Confederates on May 9, 1863.

Pier of Cheat River Bridge at Macomber, Preston County on Route 250. Built in 1835 burned in 1964. Used by both armies during the war. On April 27, 1863 Confederate General Jones's army passed over the bridge and tore up the decking on one side of the bridge. It was two years before it was repaired.

Barracksville Covered Bridge at Barracksville, Marion County. Built in 1853. It was saved from destruction by local residents pleading with Confederate General Jones who passed by here on April 29, 1863.

113

Buffington's Island in the Ohio River opposite Ravenswood, Jackson County. Scene of only battle fought in Ohio July 19, 1863 against Morgan's Raiders. Gunboats which took part in the battle were in West Virginia territory.

"Old White" at White Sulphur Springs, Greenbrier County. Built in 1854, torn down in 1913. Used as a hospital during the war. Union General Hunter was going to burn the hotel in 1864 but decided to save the building for future use. Courtesy W. Va. Dept. of Archives and History.

Site of Battle of White Sulphur Springs, Greenbrier County at junction of Routes 60 and 92. August 26, 1863.

Reenactment of the Battle of Droop Mountain at the battlefield site in Pocahontas County, Labor Day 1974. The troops are waiting for battle. Courtesy of Michael Meador, W. Va. Dept. of Natural Resources.

Droop Mountain Battlefield on Route 219 in Pocahontas County. Scene of battle November 6, 1863.

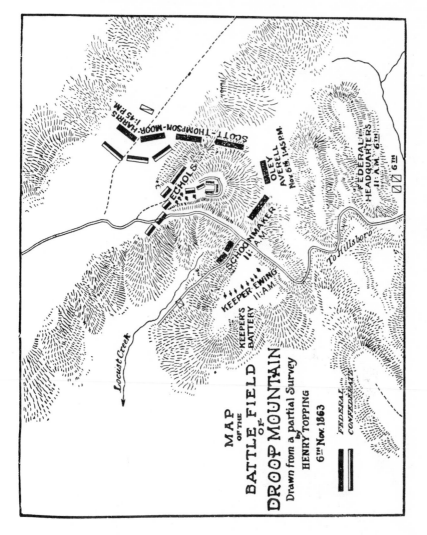

MAP
OF THE
BATTLE FIELD
OF
DROOP MOUNTAIN
Drawn from a partial Survey
by
HENRY TOPPING
6TH Nov. 1863

FEDERAL
CONFEDERATE

Locust Creek

KEEPER'S
BATTERY
KEEPER EWING
11 A.M.

SCHOONMAKER
11 A.M.

3RD
ECHOLS

SCOTT-THOMPSON-MOOR-HARRIS
1:45 P.M.

OLEY
AVERELL
Nov 6TH 1145 P.M.

FEDERAL
HEADQUARTERS
11 A.M. 6TH

6TH

To Hillsboro

From Official Records-Atlas.

Map 8

119

Remains of Fort Scammon at Fayetteville, Fayette County.

Camp of the 12th Regt. OVI at Fayetteville, Fayette County April, 1863. Courtesy of WVU Library Archives.

Site of the Bulltown Bridge over the Little Kanawha River on Route 19 in Braxton County. A fort was constructed here to guard the Weston to Gauley Bridge Turnpike. The Battle of Bulltown was fought near here on October 13, 1863.

Site of the Battle of Hurricane Bridge near Hurricane, Putnam County on Route 60. Federal forces stationed here were attacked by Confederates and withdrew to Point Pleasant after a five hour battle on March 28, 1863.

B and O Railroad Bridge across Tray Run Viaduct near Cheat River.

CHAPTER SIX

1864-65
Last Actions of the War

The last year and a half of war was mainly a period of raid and counter-raid in West Virginia with most of the larger skirmishes taking place in the eastern panhandle area. By this time the Federal forces had secured most of the new state and it was mainly a matter of keeping the "rebs" in their place and guarding the B and O Railroad. Guerrilla activity, however, continued right up until the end of the war.

Gen. John C. Breckenridge had assumed command of Confederate forces in West Virginia in March 1864, while Gen. David Hunter took over command of Union forces in May, 1864.

CROOK'S RAID

One of the largest Union raids of 1864 was Gen. George Crook's drive into Virginia to try to destroy the salt works at Saltville and to cut and destroy as much as he could of the vital Virginia and Tennessee Railroad. He was to coordinate his attack with Gen. Franz Sigel, who was to leave Martinsburg and travel up the Shenandoah Valley to meet Crook at Staunton, Virginia. Sigel was defeated soundly at the Battle of New Market, Virginia, on May 15, however, and Crook was on his own.

Crook left Charleston on May 2, 1864, and traveled through Gauley Bridge, Fayetteville, Beckley, Oceania and Princeton to Virginia. He met a Confederate force under Gen. Albert G. Jenkins at Cloyd's Mountain near Dublin, Virginia, on May 9 and defeated it. Gen. Jenkins was killed in this engagement. This was mainly a battle between West Virginia troops on both sides and both had scores to settle. The Union cavalry under Gen. Averell had gone in another direction and managed to destroy part of the railroad but not the salt works. Both Union commands met afterwards at Union, Monroe County, and went to Meadow Bluff to rest before returning to the Kanawha Valley.

GENERAL HUNTER

After the New Market battle, Gen. Hunter marched his Union army against Lynchburg, Staunton and Lexington, Virginia. At Lynchburg on June 17 he met strong resistance and thinking that Confederate Gen. Jubal Early's troops had arrived he retreated through Sweet Springs and Lewisburg, down the Kanawha River to the Ohio, and up to Parkersburg, where he entrained to Martinsburg to try again to stop Gen. Early's army. His retreat through the state had lasted a week and portions of a letter from one of his soldiers shows how the men fared in the mountains of West Virginia —

On and on we went; at last we halted. Of course we did not pitch our tents. We had dispensed with almost everything of that kind long ago. Our clothes were fast passing away. Many had worn out their shoes and were barefoot. Everything that was eatable that came in our way was eaten, such as roots and herbs. We pealed the black birch trees and ate the bark. I crippled along, stopping when I could go no farther. I thought of leaving my equipment and breaking my Springfield but finally brought them through. Their weight was about 18 pounds and they were all that we had to protect ourselves. Rations came in just before dark. The mountains ring and echo back the shouts and joy. Cheer on Cheer on now went up until we were hoarse and out of breath.

At White Sulphur Springs, Greenbrier County, on June 24 Gen. Hunter decided to burn the famous health spa hotel but was convinced by Capt. Henry A. duPont of the famous duPont family to save the buildings in case the Union forces came through again and needed them. Hunter was also thwarted in another burning in July at Martinsburg. He had ordered the burning of three homes in the eastern panhandle region in retaliation for the Confederate burning of the home of the Maryland governor. Two homes were destroyed and Boydville in Martinsburg was to be the third. Mrs. Charles Faulkner, the owner of the house, pleaded with President Lincoln, and minutes before the burning a telegram was received from him sparing the house.

Rutherford B. Hayes, who fought in West Virginia during most of the war and later became president of the United States, gave his impressions of Gen. Hunter and the "rebels" in a letter he wrote home from Charleston on July 24, 1864:

Dearest:

Back again to this point last night. Camped opposite the lower end of Camp White on the broad level bottom in the angle between Elk and Kanawha. My headquarters on one of the pretty wooded hills near Judge Summer's —

You wrote one thoughtless sentence complaining of Lincoln for failing to protect our unfortunate prisoners by retaliation. All a mistake, darling. All such things should be avoided as much as possible. We have done too much rather than too little. Gen. Hunter turned Mrs. Governor Letcher and daughter out of their home at Lexington and on 10 minutes notice burned the beautiful place in retaliation for some bushwhackers' burning out Governor Pierpont (of loyal Va.). And I am glad to say that Gen. Crook's division officers and men were all disgusted with it.....

You use the phrase "brutal Rebels." Don't be cheated in that way. There are enough "brutal Rebels" no doubt, but we have brutal officers on this raid. And there are plenty of humane Rebels. I have seen a good deal of it on this trip. War is a cruel business and there is brutality in it on all sides, but it is very idle to get up anxiety on account of any supposed peculiar cruelty on the part of Rebels. Keepers of prisons in Cincinnati, as well as in Danville, are hard-hearted and cruel.......

Affectionately
R.

GENERAL McCAUSLAND

Gen. John McCausland of Putnam County, who had taken over command at Cloyd's Mountain after Gen. Jenkins death, became famous in July, 1864 for his raid on Chambersburg, Pennsylvania. He was directed to raid Pennsylvania in retaliation for Gen. Hunter's operations in the Shenandoah Valley. He demanded a large ransom from the town and when he did not receive it he looted and burned it. He then retreated to West Virginia and stopped in the vacinity of Romney. Being flushed with a victory he decided to expand his raid and attack Keyser (New Creek) in Mineral County, and the B and O Railroad clear to the Ohio River, and then proceed to the Kanawha Valley before heading back to the east. His attempt at Keyser failed and he retreated back to Old Fields, just north of Moorefield, where he was defeated on Aug. 7 by Gen. Averell, who had been in pursuit of him from Pennsylvania. Averell captured 420 prisoners and 400 horses and retook the plunder from Chambersburg.

OTHER ACTIONS IN 1864

In other parts of the state there was also considerable action. In March, Union troops destroyed the nitrate plant above Franklin, Pendleton County, and on May 4, Capt. Jesse McNeill with 61 Confederate cavalrymen captured Piedmont, Mineral County, burning two trains and the machine shops and capturing 104 prisoners. A Confederate raid in central West Virginia in September resulted in the capture of Weston and Buckhannon. The troops were replused, however, at Winfield, Putnam County, on Oct. 26. Beverly was again attacked by 300 Confederates on Oct. 29 but they were replused by Union troops under Col. Robert Youant. The Union troops were attacked early in the morning while at roll call and in the darkness friend and foe could not be distinguished. Gen. T.L. Rosser with 2,000 Confederate troops surprised 800 Federals at Fort Fuller in Keyser on Nov. 28 and took the town, supplies and prisoners. Much of the fighting in the eastern panhandle in the late summer was a result of Gen. Early's Shenandoah Valley Campaign which threatened Washington, D.C., in an attempt to draw troops away from the battle around Petersburg, Virginia. The famous Confederate guerrilla leader John Mosby was also active in this area during the year.

During the last months of the war in 1865 the action in the state was mainly in the eastern panhandle. There two of the strangest raids of the entire war took place.

GENERALS CAPTURED

On Jan. 11, 1865, Confederate Gen. Rosser with 300 men crossed Cheat Mountain, went down the Tygart Valley, made a detour around Beverly and formed a line of battle in a hollow within 450 yards of the Union camp. The Union forces had had a dance the night before and their guard was lax. As a consequence 580 troops were captured in their quarters, marched 162 miles to Staunton, Virginia, and put on cattle cars for the trip to Richmond and prison. The Union commander, Col. Youart, was dismissed from the service after this incident.

McNEILL'S RAIDERS

Capt. McNeill and a small group of his McNeill's Rangers, a local band of southern partisans operating out of Hardy County, slipped into Cumberland, Maryland, on the night of Feb. 21 in the midst of 3,500 Union troops and captured Gens. Crook and Kelley in their hotel rooms. They slipped across the Potomac River, proceeded towards Moorefield through hundreds of enemy troops and after three days and more than 154 miles arrived in Harrisonburg, Virginia. The captured generals were sent by coach to Staunton to meet Gen Early.

At the end of the war, the few Confederate troops left in the state laid down their arms. McNeill's Rangers surrendered at Romney in April but surrendered only their old antique firearms and kept their good weapons. They were also allowed to keep the U.S. Army cavalry saddles that they had captured and used in the war. One partisan wanted to know if he could keep a little powder to go coon hunting, or maybe to hunt a Swamp Dragon (Union home guard) along the North Fork.

West Virginia had not heard the last. After the war, Virginia officially protested the loss of Berkeley and Jefferson counties in the eastern panhandle. The dispute went to the U.S. Supreme Court, which ruled in 1870 that these two counties should permanently remain in West Virginia.

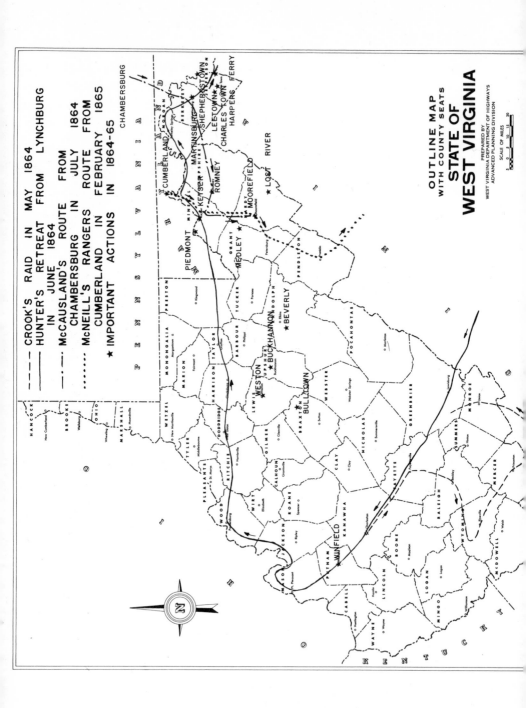

CROOK'S RAID IN MAY 1864
FROM LYNCHBURG

HUNTER'S RETREAT FROM LYNCHBURG
IN JUNE 1864

McCAUSLAND'S ROUTE FROM
CHAMBERSBURG IN JULY 1864

McNEILL'S RANGERS ROUTE FROM
CUMBERLAND IN FEBRUARY 1865

★ IMPORTANT ACTIONS IN 1864-65

OUTLINE MAP
WITH COUNTY SEATS
STATE OF
WEST VIRGINIA

PREPARED BY
WEST VIRGINIA DEPARTMENT OF HIGHWAYS
ADVANCED PLANNING DIVISION

SCALE OF MILES

Map 9

130

Boydville in Martinsburg, Berkeley County on Queen Street. Built in 1812. Saved from burning by General David Hunter in 1864 by a direct order of President Lincoln. Courtesy of Mr. and Mrs. G. Roderick Cheeseman.

Willow Wall Home at Old Fields, Hardy County on Route 220. Headquarters for McNeil's Rangers, a Confederate partisan group that operated in the area. Scene of the Battle of Moorefield August 7, 1864.

Blue Sulphur Springs Spring House in Greenbrier County, four miles south of Smoot on Route 25. All that remains of the health spa and Allegheny College which were located here. Burned by Union troops in October 1864. 89 Confederate soldiers, who died of sickness, are buried near here.

Site of Fort Moore at Glenville, Gilmer County. On hill behind Glenville State College. Built by the Gilmer Home Guards and burned in December, 1864 by Confederate troops.

OTHER POINTS
OF INTEREST

There are many other sites in the state related to the Civil War in one way or another and I have included pictures of some of them. Many houses and other buildings that were built before the war perhaps were used as barracks, headquarters, or hospitals. Let us hope that many of these buildings are preserved for future generations to search out their secrets of history.

In travel throughout the state I found many people who are not far removed from relatives who either fought in the war or at least can remember the events. General McCausland's grandson still works the original farm in Mason County. One man I talked to in Pocahontas County remembers his uncle telling him how as a child he saw General Lee when he was headquartered at Valley Mountain. There are still a few people living whose parents were living during the war and some can relate many tales told them in their youth. I strongly urge people to seek out the "old timers" and learn more of the history of this region before it all disappears. Maybe you can dig up a site lost to the memories.

Organ Cave, five miles south of Caldwell, Greenbrier County on Route 63. Confederate army made gunpowder here and supposedly held church services inside the cave.

Cleante Janutolo Spring at Fayetteville, Fayette County on Route 21. Used by both armies during the war.

Berkeley County Courthouse in Martinsburg at King and Queen Streets. Built in 1856. Records destroyed by Union troops. Belle Boyd, Confederate spy was imprisoned here several times.

Confederate General McCausland's house in Mason County on Route 35. House built in 1885. He lived here from 1885 until 1927.

Greenbottom, the home of Confederate General Albert Jenkins near Lesage, Cabell County on Route 2. Built in 1835.

Carroll (Thomas) House in Guyandotte, Cabell County next to Guyandotte River. Mrs. Carroll's pleas saved the house from burning by Federal troops on November 10, 1861.

141

Monument to the Confederate soldiers of Monroe County at Union on Route 219. Erected in 1901.

Monument to Brooker T. Washington at Malden, Kanawha County on Route 60. Born a slave in Virginia and moved to Malden after the Civil War. Worked in the salt furnaces as a youth and entered Hampton Institute in 1872. Returned to Malden in 1875 to teach for two years and then went on to build Tuskegee Institute in Alabama and become a famous educator. He died in 1915.

143

Confederate Monument at Romney, Hampshire County on Route 50. One of the oldest Confederate monuments in the south. Dedicated September 26, 1867.

Cannon in city park, Parkersburg, Wood County. Was at Fort Boreman, built in 1863 to guard the Ohio River at Parkersburg.

*Presbyterian Church at Moorefield, Hardy County on Route 220.
Built in 1847. Used as a hospital by both sides during war. Union
troops used it as a stable and the Federal Government paid $800
in damages in 1915.*

Site of Union Fort Fuller at Potomac State College in Keyser, Mineral County.

147

Old Jefferson County Courthouse in Shepherdstown, Jefferson County. Now part of Shepherd College. Used as a hospital during the war.

Halfway House at Ansted, Fayette County on old Route 60. Built in 1810 and used as the headquarters of the Chicago Grey Dragoons winter of 1861-62.

Bridge pier at Gauley Bridge, Fayette County. Bridge burned by Confederate troops on July 27, 1861. New bridge constructed on the piers and again destroyed by Federal troops in September 1862. First bridge constructed here in 1822.

Second bridge at Gauley Bridge, Fayette County. Destroyed by Union troops in September 1862. Courtesy of WVU Library Archives.

Jackson's Mill, Lewis County in the late 1800's. Courtesy of WVU Library Archives.

Jackson's Mill, Lewis County just off Route 19 near Weston. Showing the mill and site of Jackson's home (arrow). Built in 1837. Owned by West Virginia University and used as a 4-H camp.

Morris Memorial Church in Cedar Grove, Kanawha County on Route 60. Built in 1853 on site of first church in the Kanawha Valley. Used as a hospital by Confederate troops and as a stable by Union troops. $700 was paid to the church after the war for damages done by the Union troops.

Craiks-Patton House at Daniel Boone Park in Charleston, Kanawha County on Route 60. The house was built in 1835 and bought by George Patton in 1858. He was a Confederate officer and grandfather of General George S. Patton of WW II fame. House has been moved to the park and is being restored by the Society of Colonial Dames of America.

Buffalo Academy in Buffalo, Putnam County. Built in 1849. Used as a hospital during the war. Confederate General McCausland attended school here.

Milton Bridge in Milton, Cabell County just of Route 60. Guarded by Union troops and scene of skirmish near here April 5, 1863.

Pier of Fetterman Covered Bridge across Tygart Valley River at Grafton, Taylor County on Route 50. Used by both armies. Built in 1835, destroyed by flood 1888.

Jackson family cemetery in Clarksburg, Harrison County on Route 50. Contains most of the relatives of General Stonewall Jackson's family.

Grafton National Cemetery located in Grafton, Taylor County. Only National Cemetery in the state, established in 1868 and contains 1200 soldiers of the Civil War.

Old jail at Pruntytown, Taylor County on Route 50. The first slaves released in the United States by the order of President Lincoln were freed here on November 22, 1862. The slaves were kept here to keep them from joining the Union forces and the President declared them "contraband of war." Now part of the Boys school at Pruntytown.

Site of Union Fort Pendleton in Maryland facing Gormania, Grant County on Route 50. Fort used to guard the Northwestern Turnpike. Arrows point to trenches.

Weston State Hospital in Weston, Lewis County. First called Trans-Allegheny Lunatic Asylum when the three one story wings were started in 1858. The asylum was opened in 1864 and is the largest hand cut stone building in the country. This asylum and a few roads were all that the new state of West Virginia took over from Virginia on June 20, 1863.

Fort Mullegan at Petersburg, Grant County on Route 28. Constructed by the Union Army. Picture shows remains of breastworks.

Site of Fort Pickens at Duffy, Lewis County, two miles east of Ireland on Route 19. Company A, 10th W. Va. Volunteer Infantry built fort for their headquarters in 1861-62. It was burned in 1864.

165

Literary Hall, Romney, Hampshire County. Built in 1825, destroyed in 1862. It has been completely reconstructed. Oldest library building in the state.

Remaining cottages and ruins of the Erskine House at Salt Sulphur Springs, Monroe County on Route 219. A famous health spa built in the 1830's and used as a headquarters and hospital during the war. General Jenkins left on his raid from here in 1862. General Averell quartered his sick here after the Battle of Droop Mountain.

Erskine House, Salt Sulphur Springs, Monroe County. Photo taken after the Civil War. Courtesy Dr. Margaret Ballard, Union, W. Va.

Original buildings at Salt Sulphur Springs, Monroe County.

Main building, Andrew S. Rowan Memorial Home, Sweet Springs, Monroe County. Designed by Thomas Jefferson and was a well known health spa in the 1800's. Courtesy Dr. Margaret Ballard, Union, W. Va.

PERSONALITIES
NORTH AND SOUTH

Many thousands of West Virginians served in the armies of the North and South, and the state provided ten generals for the Union army and four for the Confederate. Some of the personalities who helped shape the history of the state during the war are described below.

GENERAL WILLIAM W. AVERELL (1832-1900): Commander of Union forces in northern West Virginia in May 1863, and commander at the battles of Droop Mountain and Moorefield. Led several raids in West Virginia, the most notable being the raid on Salem, Virginia, in December 1863. After the war was counsul-general to Canada and president of a large manufacturing company.

ARTHUR I. BOREMAN (1823-96): Born in Pennsylvania but moved to Tyler County and became a lawyer and a member of the Virginia Assembly. Presided over the Second Wheeling Convention in June 1861. Elected first governor of the new state of West Virginia and took office June 20, 1863, serving until 1869. Was then elected to the United States Senate and afterwards returned to Parkersburg to practice law. Was appointed a judge in 1888.

GENERAL JACOB D. COX (1828-1900): Ohio commander of the "Brigade of the Kanawha" at the beginning of the war and Union commander at the Battle of Scary Creek in July 1861. Head of the Department of the Kanawha until August 1862. After the Battle of Antietam was commander of West Virginia forces until April 1863. Fought the remainder of the war in the western campaigns. Governor of Ohio 1867 -69 and Secretary of the Interior 1869-70.

GENERAL GEORGE CROOK (1829-90): Colonel of the 36th Ohio in West Virginia operations in 1861 and commander of Union forces at the Battle of Lewisburg May 23, 1862. Commanded the Kanawha Division at the Battles of South Mountain and Antietam. Fought in West Virginia September 1862 to February 1863 and was the commander of the Kanawha District in February 1864. Led a raid on the Virginia and Tennessee Railroad in May 1864 and fought at the Battle of Cloyd's Mountain. Succeeded General Hunter as commander of Department of West Virginia in August 1864. Led Army of West Virginia in Sheridan's Shenandoah Valley campaign in 1864. One of the two generals captured at Cumberland, Maryland, in 1865. Became a famous Indian fighter after the war.

GENERAL JOHN ECHOLS (1823-96): Born in Virginia but lived and practiced law in Union, Monroe County. Succeeded Gen. Loring in October, 1862, as commander of Confederate troops in the Kanawha Valley. Commander at the Battle of Droop Mountain in November, 1863, and fought with Gen. Early in the Shenandoah Valley Campaign in 1864. After Lee's surrender escorted President Jefferson Davis on his flight from Richmond.

GENERAL JOHN FLOYD (1806-63): Confederate general, Governor of Virginia and President Buchanan's Secretary of War. Commander of forces under Gen. Lee in his West Virginia campaign in 1861 and commander at the Battle of Carnifex Ferry in September 1861.

GENERAL JOHN FREMONT (1813-80): Union general. Famous as a western explorer before the war and elected governor of California in 1846. Republican nominee for President in 1856. Commander of Union forces in Missouri 1861-62 and in West Virginia March to June 1862, when he was relieved of his command.

NANCY HART: A girl guerrilla from Roane County, who fought with the Moccasin Rangers, a Confederate partisan group in central West Virginia. Spied on Union troops and was captured and imprisoned at Summersville in Nicholas County. Escaped and led Confederate troops back to Summersville where they drove the Union forces from the town. Married a former Ranger and lived in Greenbrier County until she died in 1902.

RUTHERFORD B. HAYES (1822-93): Nineteenth President of the United States. Entered the war with the 23rd Ohio Regiment and fought in many battles in West Virginia and the Virginia Valley. Attained the rank of Brevet general.

GENERAL HENRY HETH (1825-99): Confederate general who fought with General Lee in his 1861 campaign and commanded at the Battle of Lewisburg in May 1862. Fought the rest of the war with the Army of Northern Virginia and was in the insurance business in Richmond after the war.

GENERAL DAVID HUNTER (1802-86): Union general. Fought in Missouri at the beginning of the war and liberated all the slaves under his command in 1862. President Lincoln annulled his orders on grounds he had exceeded his authority. Hunter took over the Department of West Virginia in May 1864. He was repulsed by Gen. Early at Lynchburg in June 1864, and retreated into West Virginia leaving Washington, D.C., open to attack. He gave up his command on Aug. 8, 1864, and was labeled a "felon to be executed if captured" by President Jefferson Davis for his violent acts in Virginia and West Virginia. After the war ended he presided over the commission that tried Lincoln's assassination conspirators.

GENERAL JOHN D. IMBODEN (1823-95): Confederate general and one of the leaders of the Jones-Imboden Raid through West Virginia in the spring of 1863. Fought at Gettysburg and with General Early in his Valley campaign in Virginia and West Virginia in 1864. Became a lawyer and land developer in Virginia after the war.

GENERAL T.J. (STONEWALL) JACKSON (1824-63):
General in the Confederate army. Born in Clarksburg, Harrison
County, and spent 12 years of his childhood at Jackson's Mill,
Lewis County. Attended West Point, fought in the Mexican War
and taught at Virginia Military Institute. Witnessed John
Brown's hanging at Charles Town. Commander of troops at
Harpers Ferry in 1861 and 1862 and was in charge of the capture
of railroad equipment at Martinsburg in May 1861. Conducted
Valley campaign in Virginia and West Virginia in the spring of
1862. Killed at the Battle of Chancellorsville on May 10, 1863, by
mistake of his own men. He is buried at Lexington, Virginia.

Jackson's only sister Laura married an ardent secessionist and
moved to Beverly, Randolph County, but was loyal to the Union
cause throughout the war. This produced many problems in her
household.

GENERAL ALBERT GALLATIN JENKINS (1830-64):
Confederate general was born at Greenbottom, Cabell County.
Graduated from Harvard Law School and practiced in
Charleston. Elected a representative to the Confederate
Congress from western Virginia. Fought under Gen. Floyd in the
Kanawha Valley and led a raid through central West Virginia in
1862. Led an advanced guard into Pennsylvania before Lee's
invasion in 1863. Commander of forces at the Battle of Cloyd's
Mountain, May 9, 1864, where he was killed.

GENERAL WILLIAM E. JONES (1824-64): Confederate
general. Led part of the Jones-Imboden raid in April-May, 1863.
Killed at the Battle of Piedmont June 5, 1864.

GENERAL BENJAMIN FRANKLIN KELLEY (1807-91):
From Wheeling, Ohio County. Commander of Union forces at the
Battle of Philippi June 3, 1861. Spent most of the war in the state
defending the B and O Railroad. He was captured at Cumberland,
Maryland, in January 1865, by McNeill's Rangers and held at
Richmond. Was in government service after the war.

GENERAL ROBERT E. LEE (1807-70): Leading Confederate
general of the war and commander of forces in West Virginia
August to October 1861. Commander of the Army of Northern
Virginia 1862-65. His campaign in West Virginia was a failure
and the Union forces kept control of most of the state during the
war.

GENERAL JOSEPH A.J. LIGHTBURN (1824-1901): Union general. Born in Lewis County and a boyhood friend of Stonewall Jackson. Delegate to the Second Wheeling Convention. Took part in campaigns in the Kanawha Valley and was driven from there by Gen. Loring's Confederate army in September 1862. Served during the rest of the war with Generals Grant and Sherman. Became a Baptist minister after the war.

GENERAL WILLIAM W. LORING (1818-86): Confederate general and a soldier most of his life. Lost an arm in the Mexican War and fought in many campaigns until the beginning of the Civil War when he sided with the South. Commander of Lee's forces in the Cheat Mountain campaign in 1861 and at Romney, Hampshire County, under Stonewall Jackson in January 1862. Captured the Kanawha Valley in September, 1862 but occupied the area only one and a half months. Relieved of command in October 1862 and fought the remainder of the war in the lower South.

GENERAL JOHN McCAUSLAND (1836-1927): Confederate general was gorn in St. Louis, Missouri. Moved to Mason County as a youth and attended Buffalo Academy at Buffalo, Putnam County. Also attended and taught at Virginia Military Institute. Witnessed the hanging of John Brown at Charles Town. Fought with Gen. Floyd in West Virginia in 1861 and then joined forces in Kentucky and at Fort Donelson, Tennessee, where he escaped before the Confederate surrender. Served in West Verginia, 1862-64, to protect the Virginia and Tennessee Railroad. Delayed Gen. Hunter at Lynchburg, Virginia, in 1864 and saved the city. Defeated Gen. Lew Wallace in Maryland in 1864 and rode to the outskirts of Washington, D.C. Led the raid on Chambersburg, Pennsylvania, in 1864 and was defeated at the Battle of Moorefield, Hardy County, Aug. 7, 1864. Was with Gen. Lee at Appomattox but his brigade refused to surrender and escaped. Traveled to Europe and Mexico for two years and then returned to the Kanawha River in Mason County to live the rest of his life. He was one of two high ranking Confederate officers left when he died at age 91, still insisting he was an "unreconstructed and unregenerate rebel."

GENERAL GEORGE B. McCLELLAN (1826-85): Commander of Ohio troops at the beginning of the war and of Union troops in West Virginia from the beginning of the war until July 22, 1861, when he was called to Washington to assume overall command of the Union army. Commander in the Peninsular Campaign and the Battle of Antietam, and Democratic presidential candidate in 1864. He was an engineer after the war.

WILLIAM McKINLEY (1843-1901): Twenty-fourth President of the United States. Entered the army as a private in the 23rd Ohio Regiment and attained the rank of major. Fought in many battles in West Virginia and the Virginia Valley.

COLONEL GEORGE S. PATTON: Confederate officer from Charleston, Kanawha County. Grandfather of World War II Gen. George S. Patton. Formed the "Kanawha Riflemen" in Charleston which became part of the 22nd Virginia Infantry Regiment. Fought at Scary Creek, Carnifex Ferry, White Sulphur Springs, Lewisburg, Droop Mountain, and New Market, and was killed at the Battle of Winchester on Sept. 19, 1864.

FRANCIS H. PIERPONT (1814-99): Born in Monongalia County. Lawyer and a leader in the formation of the State of West Virginia. His plan was used to set up the Restored Government of Virginia, and was elected its governor at the Second Wheeling Convention in June, 1861. After the new state was admitted to the Union moved his government to Alexandria, Virginia, and then to Richmond at the end of the war. Was removed from office in 1867 because he was accused of being too conciliatory to the State of Virginia.

GENERAL JESSE LEE RENO (1823-62): Born in Wheeling, Ohio County. The highest ranking Union officer from West Virginia. Fought in Virginia and was killed at the Battle of South Mountain in September 1862.

GENERAL JOHN J. REYNOLDS (1822-99): Union commander of the Cheat Mountain District under Gen. Rosecrans in 1861. Fought in the western campaigns until the end of the war. A well-known Indian fighter after the war.

GENERAL WILLIAM S. ROSECRANS (1819-98): Union general on Gen. McClellan's staff in West Virginia April to June, 1861, and commander of Union forces at the Battles of Rich Mountain and Carnifex Ferry. Fought until the end of the war in the western campaigns. A congressman and rancher after the war.

GENERAL DAVID HUNTER STROTHER (1816-88): Born in Martinsburg, Berkeley County. A general in the Union army. Fought in Virginia and Lousiana and with his cousin Gen. David Hunter in the Virginia Valley campaign in 1864. Well-known during the war as a correspondent and artist for Harpers Weekly Magazine using the pen name "Porte Crayon."

GENERAL HENRY WISE (1806-76): Confederate general and former governor of Virginia. Commander of Confederate forces in the Kanawha Valley area in July 1861, and under Gen. Lee in his West Virginia campaign until relieved of command in September 1861. Surrendered with Gen. Lee at Appomattox in April 1865.

Governor Arthur I. Boreman

General William W. Averell

General George Crook.

General Jacob D. Cox.

179

General John B. Floyd. Courtesy W. Va. Dept. of Archives and History.

John Echols, Colonel of a "Stonewall" Regiment at Bull Run; Later Led a Brigade in Lee's Army.

General John Echols

Nancy Hart.

General Robert S. Garnett.
Courtesy W. Va. Hillbilly.

General David Hunter.

General Henry Heth

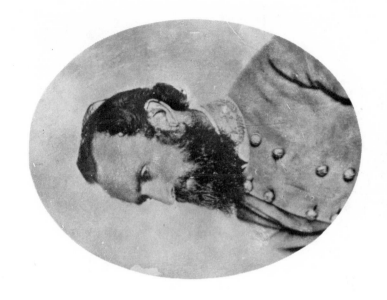

General Stonewall Jackson.
Courtesy WVU Library Archives.

General John D. Imboden

General B.F. Kelley

General Albert G. Jenkins.
Courtesy WVU Library Archives.

General Joseph A.J. Lightburn.
Courtesy W. Va. Dept. of Archives and History.

General Robert E. Lee as he looked in 1861.
Courtesy W. Va. Dept. of Archives and History.

General John McCausland.
Courtesy W. Va. Dept. of Archives and History.

General W. W. Loring.

Colonel George S. Patton.

General George B. McClellan.
Courtesy W. Va. Dept. of Archives and History.

General Jesse Lee Reno.

Governor Francis H. Pierpont.
Courtesy W. Va. Dept. of Archives and History.

General William S. Rosecrans.
Courtesy W. Va. Dept. of Archives and History.

General John J. Reynolds

General Henry A. Wise.

General David Strother.
Courtesy W. Va. Dept. of Archives and History.

BIBLIOGRAPHY

Ambler, Charles H., *West Virginia, the Mountain State*, Prentice-Hall, New York, 1940.

Ambler, Charles H., *West Virginia Stories & Biographies*, Rand McNalley & Co., New York, 1937.

Boatner, Mark Mayo *The Civil War Dictionary*, D. McKay Co., New York, 1959.

Conley, Phil and Doherty, William Thomas, *West Virginia History*, Education Foundation Inc., Charleston, W. Va., 1974.

Conley, Phil, *West Virginia a Brief History of The Mountain State*, Centennial 1863-1963.

Cometti, Elizabeth and Summers, Festus P., *The 35th State, A Documentary History of West Virginia*, McClain Printing Co., Parsons, W. Va., 1966.

Duffey, J.W., *Two Generals Kidnaped*, Moorefield Examiner, Moorefield, W. Va., 1944.

Hendricks, Sam, *Military Operations in Jefferson County, Va. (and W. Va.)*, Shepherdstown, W. Va., 1910.

Hornbeck, Betty, *Upshur Brothers of the Blue and Gray*, McClain Printing Co., Parsons, W. Va., 1967.

McCormick, Kyle, *A Story of the Formation of West Virginia*, W. Va. Dept. of Archives and History, Charleston, W. Va., 1961.

McCormick, Kyle, *The New River-Kanawha River and the Mine War of West Virginia*, Matthews Printing Co., Charleston, W. Va., 1959.

Selected Archeological and Historical Sites in West Virginia, Preliminary Plan for Development, Wheeling College, 1965.

Stutler, Boyd B., *West Virginia in the Civil War*, Education Foundation Inc., Charleston, W. Va., 1963.

Summers, Festus P., *The Baltimore and Ohio in the Civil War*, G. P. Putnam, New York, 1939.

Writers Program WPA, *West Virginia – A Guide to the Mountain State*, Oxford University Press, New York, 1941.

Plus many other booklets, pamphlets and newspapers.

INDEX

G

Garnett, Gen. Robert S., 19, 21, 22
Gauley Bridge, 21, 23, 83, 84, 125
Gauley River, 84
Gettysburg, 105, 173
Glenville, 83
Grafton, 16, 17, 18, 19, 105, 106
Grant Co., 106
Greenbrier Co., 7, 21, 24, 82, 108, 126, 173
Greenbrier River, 24, 82, 110
Greenbrier Valley, 110
Greenbottom, 174
Greenland Gap, Battle, 106
Guyandotte, 25, 83

H

Hampshire Co., 8, 25, 81, 175
Hanger, J.E., 19
Hancock, Md.,, 81
Harper, Adam, 107
Harpers Ferry, 1, 16, 17, 83, 174
Harrison Co., 19, 174
Harrisonburg, Va., 129
Hart, David, 19
Hart, Nancy, 173
Hawks Nest, 21
Hayes, Col. Rutherford B., 82, 127, 173
Heth, Gen. Henry, 82, 173
Hill, Gen. A.P., 83
Humphreys, Sgt. Milton, 106, 107
Hunter, Gen. David, 125, 126, 127, 128, 172, 173, 175, 177
Huntersville, 108
Huttonsville, 15, 23
Huttonsville-Huntersville Pike, 23

I

Imboden, Gen. John D., 105, 106, 109, 173
Indiana, 109

J

Jackson Co., 109
Jackson, Laura, 174
Jackson, Gen. T.J. (Stonewall), 1, 17, 81, 83, 174, 175
Jackson, Gen. William L., 107
Jackson's Mill, 174
James River and Kanawha Turnpike, 15, 24, 82, 84, 108
Jefferson Co., 1, 8, 25, 83, 109, 129
Jenkins, Gen. Albert G., 82, 125, 127, 174
Johnston, Gen. Joseph, 81
Jones, Gen. William E., 105, 106, 173, 174

K

Kanawha, 7, 24
Kanawha Co., 20, 84
Kanawha River, 21, 126, 127
Kanawha, Salines, 86

Kanawha Valley, 15, 17, 20, 21, 23, 24, 25, 82, 83, 84, 126, 128, 172, 175, 177
Kanawha Valley Star, 20
Kelley, Co. Benjamin, 19, 25, 129, 174
Kentucky, 109, 175
Kesslers Cross Lanes, Battle, 24
Keyser, 110, 128
Knoxville, Tenn., 110

L

Lacey Springs, Va., 106
Laurel Hill, 19
Lee, Gen. Robert E., 1, 18, 19, 22, 23, 24, 83, 84, 105, 106, 135, 172, 173, 174, 175, 177
Letcher, Gov. John, 15, 81, 127
Lewis Co., 83, 106, 174
Lewisburg, 24, 82, 85, 108, 110, 126, 172, 173, 176
Lexington, Va., 126, 127, 174
Lightburn, Gen. Joseph A.J., 83, 84, 175
Lincoln, Pres. Abraham, 1, 5, 7, 83, 127, 173
Little Kanawha River, 106
Logan Co., 82
Loring, Gen. William W., 23, 81, 83, 84, 85, 172, 175
Loudoun Heights, 83
Lynchburg, Va., 126, 173, 175

M

Mace, 23
Marion Co., 106
Marlinton, 108
Marmet, 84
Martinsburg, 125, 126, 127, 174, 177
Maryland, 1, 16, 19, 81, 83, 105, 127, 172, 174
Maryland Heights, 83
Mason Co., 83, 135, 175
McCausland, Gen. John, 127, 135, 175
McDowell Co., 7
McKinley, H. William, 82, 176
McLaws, Gen. Layayette, 83
McClellan, Gen. George, 17, 19, 20, 23, 83, 175, 177
McNeill, Capt. Jesse, 128, 129
McNeill's Rangers, 129, 174
Meadow Bluff, 24, 126
Mercer Co., 7, 82
Miles, Col. Dixon, 83
Milroy, Gen. Robert, 25, 107, 108
Mineral Co., 110, 128
Monongahela River, 106
Monongalia Co., 106, 176
Monroe Co., 7, 82, 86, 109, 126, 172
Monterey, Va., 19
Moorefield, 106, 128, 129, 171, 175
Morgan, Gen. John, 109
Morgan Co., 8, 81
Morgantown, 106
Morris Harvey College, 84
Mosby, John, 128
Mount Vernon, 23